Penguin Education

Management and the Social Sciences

Tom Lupton

Tom Lupton

Management and the Social Sciences

Third Edition

Penguin Books

Penguin Books Ltd, Harmondsworth, Middlesex, England
Penguin Books, 40 West 23rd Street, New York, New York 10010, U.S.A.
Penguin Books Australia Ltd, Ringwood, Victoria, Australia
Penguin Books Canada Ltd, 2801 John Street, Markham, Ontario, Canada L3R 1B4
Penguin Books (N.Z.) Ltd, 182–190 Wairau Road, Auckland 10, New Zealand

First published by Lyon, Grant Green Ltd 1966
Second edition published in Penguin Books 1971
Reprinted 1972, 1974, 1975, 1976, 1978, 1980
Third edition 1983

Copyright © The Administrative Staff College, 1966
Copyright © Tom Lupton, 1971, 1983

Made and printed in Singapore by
Richard Clay (S.E. Asia) Pte Ltd

Set in Linotron 202 Times

Contents

Preface

This essay has two main objectives: firstly, to introduce the social science of organizations to those managers who have no previous knowledge of it and to others such as students coming fresh to the study of management; and secondly, to dispel such scepticism as may exist amongst those outside the social sciences who have already encountered their methods and findings. Those two objectives have not changed since the first edition was published, but the content has been enlarged and amended so as to encompass changes both in the issues that perplex managers and in the concerns and methods of social scientists.

Chapter 1 describes and analyses the job of the manager and defines those aspects of the methods and findings of the social sciences which are relevant to the understanding of that job, and its effective performance.

Chapter 2 is mainly a history of ideas. It describes early attempts by social scientists and managers to understand the nature of modern industrial and commercial organizations, and to find ways to put that knowledge to practical use.

Chapter 3 summarizes and comments upon some of the better known recent research in organizations carried out by social scientists in North America and Europe. These examples are chosen to illustrate the methods of social science and to display the knowledge that has been accumulating about organizations treated as social systems. They also show how far the theories and insights described in Chapter 2 have stood the test of detailed and systematic observation of human beings in organizational habitats.

Chapter 4 considers more specifically what social science has to offer to the manager by referring to some practical problems that managers face, e.g. the management of conflict, the management of change, and the management of communication. The chapter sets out to show that social science can be an aid to general understanding of the complexities of human organizations, and shows how social science knowledge can be turned to more immediate practical advantage.

Chapter 5 refers to some recent theoretical developments and examines their possible relevance for the practice of management.

The new material which has been added in this edition is mostly to be found in Chapters 1 and 5. However, the other chapters have been added to and amended to take account of recent developments.

Acknowledgements

The first edition of *Management and the Social Sciences* was written at the request of Mr Martin-Bates, then Principal of the Administrative Staff College at Henley, to meet an urgent need in the work of management development at the College. Naturally, I turned to my sponsors for guidance on what should be included and what left out, and on the suitability of my proposed treatment of the subject for the audience they had in mind. Two members of the College, Andrew Life and Morris Brodie, suggested valuable improvements as I worked towards a final draft. When the time came to prepare a second edition, they were just as generous with suggestions for additions and amendments. The general structure and presentation that emerged has stood the test of time and of exposure to a much wider and more varied audience than was originally envisaged, and I still remain much in debt to them for their help.

My knowledge about management and my development as a social scientist has been greatly influenced by colleagues who have worked with me over the years in the Organization Design Research Unit at the Manchester Business School. They will recognize in this edition ideas and approaches that grew out of our collaboration, the exact origins of which are difficult to attribute. I have to mention especially Dan Gowler, Karen Legge, Angela Bowey, Allan Warmington and Ian Tanner. The many managers who worked with the Unit on action research projects and consultancy work have also contributed much to the way I now look at management and its problems. Tom Clayton of Pilkington Brothers Ltd was, and is, a stimulating co-worker from whom I have learned much.

My wider debt to scholars in the world community of social science will be obvious from the text, even though their views may differ from mine. I trust that those I have briefly cited will find that

I have accurately represented their work, and where I have criticized will find what I have said constructive. It is hardly necessary to add that no one I have mentioned is responsible for my errors and omissions.

I am also grateful to the following for permission to quote extracts: the University of Chicago Press for the quotation from a paper by Chester Barnard in the *Journal of Business*; Harvard University Press for the quotations from *Management and the Worker* by Professor F. J. Roethlisberger and W. J. Dickson; Her Majesty's Stationery Office and Miss Joan Woodward for the extract from *Management and Technology*; Oliver & Boyd Ltd and Professor Max Gluckman for a quotation from *Closed Systems and Open Minds*; Prentice-Hall Inc., Dean Cyert and Professor March for comments on the economists' theory of the firm taken from *A Behavioral Theory of the Firm*; Tavistock Publications Ltd and A. K. Rice for a note on a conceptual framework elaborated in *The Enterprise and its Environment*.

I believe a good deal of conflicting bunk is taught in these fields. This argues for improvement and development, not against teaching what can be taught. In the time of Newton, or even much later, a great deal of modern physics, and much that is fundamental in it, was not known, and for this reason perhaps a good deal of bunk was then taught in that field.

CHESTER BARNARD

Introduction to the Third Edition

This book was originally written for managers to explain to them what the social sciences were. It was expected that managers would find the research findings and ideas of social scientists interesting and possibly of practical use. At the very least a knowledge of the relevant social sciences would diminish some of the scepticism that was known to exist at that time. The new revisions and additions are broadly in line with that original aim; generally managers have accepted the social sciences, but there is still a good deal of scepticism.

However, it is no longer necessary to assume, as I did then, that the needs of the manager for social scientific knowledge are obvious. Previous editions took it for granted that because managers work with people in organizations, and social scientists are known to observe and to theorize about people in organizations, what social scientists write ought to command the attention of managers, provided that it is interpreted and communicated intelligibly, and with due regard for the concerns of the audience. What those concerns might be was not made explicit, for example there was little reference to what aspects of the manager's job would require social science ideas and techniques for their successful performance. In the intervening years, social scientists have systematically observed and analysed managerial work and it is now possible to propose some answers to questions about what managers need from the social sciences in order to be more effective. In this edition, the findings of some significant recent work on the manager's job will be reported and their significance assessed.

In preparing this edition, I have also questioned the too glib assumption that the worlds of the manager and the worlds of the social scientist must of necessity be separate not only in location but also in the problems that the two groups consider interesting and worthwhile addressing, in the language used to communicate, and in the rewards for performance. It was because the worlds were considered separate there was thought to be a need for an interpreter, preferably someone who had worked in both. I am not sure that I can now accept the separation as entirely necessary, and many others have questioned the value of doing so. In my own case it is probably the result of my work as a business school teacher/researcher, which directed my attention to the practical utility and theoretical benefit to be gained from joint ventures in which both social scientists and managers are involved. It is too easy for social scientists to excuse themselves from involvement in the affairs of management on the grounds that it is their special competence to advance knowledge, and not to worry about how that knowledge will be used and who will use it, and for managers to excuse themselves from intellectual effort in the expectation that someone will make new social science knowledge available in the form of immediately usable techniques. I am not arguing that there should be no pursuit of knowledge, as a specialized activity, nor am I saying that managers should be continually reflecting on the implicit theory that governs their practical actions. However, there are occasions when the pursuit of knowledge, the solving of practical problems and mutual learning, can be combined in the same activity, and methods have been evolved for making this happen successfully. Some of these are referred to in this edition, with examples.

From the experience of joint activity has come the idea that some social scientists might become specialized in the development of generally applicable means of approaching the problems which managers generally face. Two examples of this were referred to briefly in previous editions, a procedure for choosing a payment system, and another for designing an organization structure to 'fit' a particular set of circumstances. In this edition the procedure for organization design has been improved and is set out in more detail, and three new procedures are described, one for effecting a reconciliation between economic and social/psychological objectives in the design of manufacturing systems and the others for planning organizational changes, and for introducing new technology into offices.

The future of the social science of organizations surely lies in the fruitful combination of the methods of the social scientist and the insights and experience of practitioners in management. Some portents of that future are with us now.

1

The Social Sciences and the
Nature of Management

Social science certainly includes sociology, social anthropology, social psychology and political science. Some other branches of psychology and also economics might well be included. If I were asked for a brief personal definition of social science I would include all activities which are concerned systematically to investigate and to explain aspects of the relation between the individual and the society of which he is a part. All the fields of study mentioned rest on a belief that there are regularities in social life which may be observed and which have causes which may be discovered, just as there are regularities in the physical world which are the concern of the so-called physical sciences. Each social science chooses to abstract from the complex processes of social life different relations between events, and to approach the study of them using different methods. Gluckman, a distinguished social anthropologist, has put it like this:

> The different social and behavioural sciences are in the main distinguished not by the events they study, but by the kind of relation between events that they seek to establish. Events themselves are neutral to the different disciplines (1964, page 160).

What, then, do the different social sciences study? Economists are chiefly interested in the problems of rational choice between economic alternatives in situations of scarcity, uncertainty and risk. Social psychologists study the problems arising for individuals from their membership of small social groups. Sociologists are concerned chiefly with the structuring and interlocking of social roles at work, in the family, the factory, the residential community and other bits of society, and the associated problems of social order. Social anthropologists look at the same problems – usually, but not always, in non-industrialized societies – and employ somewhat different methods of inquiry and analysis. Political scientists are interested in questions of power in society, its origins, and how it is legitimated and administered.

There are obvious areas of overlap between the various social sciences, but it is easy to see how all of them might come to be interested in industrial organizations. In industry there are problems of maintaining social order which are of interest to the political scientist and the sociologist, problems arising in relationships between social groups which attract the sociologist and the social anthropologist, and problems of the adjustment of the individual to the group which the social psychologist might wish to investigate. Then there is the effect of the physical environment on the health and well-being of the employee. This, and its influence on industrial relationships, is investigated by a branch of psychology known as industrial psychology.

The various social sciences all take as a subject for study one or other aspect of the same complex reality. Reality is, as it were, taken apart for the purpose of study, and the industrial firm is a good place to study many of its aspects. But it would seem that for the manager, or the trade-union official – the practical administrator – reality is all of a piece and has to be dealt with as such. Any one of their administrative activities might pose, at one and the same time, problems of rational choice between economic alternatives, problems of inter-group relations, problems of structure, power and authority, and problems of personal idiosyncrasy. In point of fact, managers do not deal with complex reality as a whole. When they try to theorize and to explain behaviour, they do what social scientists do: they break up reality into compartments; and when they act, they act from partial theories – as practical economists, for example, or practical psychologists.

The problems managers face rarely fall neatly within the boundaries of any one social science. This is one reason why managers are often attracted more by usable rules of thumb and practical procedures than by the social scientists' efforts to explain aspects of complex reality.

It is because the reality of social life is so complex as to defy the efforts of theorists and practical men fully to understand and explain it, that our knowledge of the behaviour of human beings individually and collectively is of necessity fragmented and in consequence difficult to apply. There are two courses open. Either we give up trying to understand and explain and rely exclusively and riskily on practical personal flair, or we seek better ways to understand and to explain, and to make our understandings and explanations available for practical men to use. This latter activity is, as I see it, the social role of social science.

Not all social scientists are interested in the problems of industrial organization, but during the last seven or eight decades, the emergence of large-scale industrial organizations of increasing complexity has attracted social scientists in greater numbers to the study of their problems. On the whole, the interest of economists in the problems of decision making *within* organizations is recent in origin. The psychologists were the first in the field and their concern was then largely with the effect of physical environment. Then came social psychology and sociology. Only very recently have political scientists begun to take an interest. The social anthropologists, especially in the USA, have long worked on industrial problems. As a result of all this work the possibility now exists of a social science of organization which will draw upon the methods and findings of all the social sciences.

In Chapter 5 of this book we shall consider the progress, or lack of it, that has been made towards this objective.

The range of problems all these social scientists have studied and written about is really quite narrow and easy to comprehend. They relate to the difficulties for human individuals and groups which arise from working in organizations and from trying to make organizations work more effectively. Industrial social scientists are interested particularly in:

1. The consequences of various ways of allocating and distributing work and authority, i.e. in problems of structure.
2. The nature of conflict and cooperation in organizations and their relation to structure.
3. Human motivation, satisfaction and incentives.
4. The communication of ideas, orders and information.
5. Physical and mental health and its relation to the physical and social environment of the individual.
6. Technical and administrative change.

At the level of common sense and general public knowledge there seems little doubt that these interests match well some of the practical concerns of management, and much that is taught in courses of study for managers reflects that certainty. Yet it would be unwise to neglect the existence of detailed evidence about the nature of management, which will enable us to say just how good the match is. In a book about management and the social sciences it is not enough to specify the present and continuing interests of social scientists, even of those who have chosen people in organizations as their field of study. Nor is it enough simply to assert the existence of a connection between what social scientists find interesting and what managers will find useful. This is because the procedures employed for acquiring and diffusing new knowledge in the social sciences have a different logical structure from those needed to manage, say, an engineering assembly plant or a municipal transport undertaking. The 'problems' the social scientist starts with are puzzles that seem to require unravelling and explaining – questions of the 'why?' variety; and his observations are structured in ways which address those questions. The 'problems' of the manager are practical difficulties requiring practical solutions. The 'answers' provided by social scientists are communicated to other social scientists and are judged by them. The 'answers' of the manager are decisions to act in certain ways to resolve difficulties. Therefore, it is surely open to question whether what social scientists say and write will always be seen as, and will actually turn out to be, relevant and useful to managers. It is worthwhile therefore to reflect briefly on the nature of management, and on the knowledge and competence required for its effective performance. This will enable us to judge a little better whether and, if so, to what extent the social sciences could be relevant to managers.

Management work and managers' skills

Management is what managers do during their working hours. Generally speaking the manager's job is to decide what is to be done (within the limits of formal authority), then to mobilize and deploy the material and human resources required to do it. He or she must then make sure that the task is completed and take responsibility for the outcome. The job of the manager obviously requires certain competences and qualities e.g. technical knowledge, social skill, intelligence, ability to think straight, commitment, motivation and self-control, as well as an understanding of the working of human organizations.

With a few notable exceptions, social scientists have shown little interest in the detailed nature of managerial work. Still fewer have addressed the question: What competences does managerial work require, which of them are most closely associated with high performance and how can social science contribute? The reasons for this relative neglect are not far to seek. Social scientists have traditionally been reluctant to become identified with any particular group in society, in case the objectivity of the social sciences be called into question. Much the same reasons have led them to fight shy of prescribing improvements, and implementing or helping to implement them; that would be social engineering, not social science. The engagement of social scientists in social engineering is relatively recent and is still relatively uncommon, but is growing. As a result, the prescriptions for effective management have come mostly from articulate practitioners, for example Taylor, Urwick, Sloan, Barnard and Brown, and not from social scientists, although some of these have been strongly influenced by social science and social scientists. The social scientists who *have* become professionally interested in the study of organization and management have been concerned more with the scholarly development and diffusion of factually based general ideas. This book was originally written because it was believed that these general ideas might usefully contribute to the competences of the manager, if they were presented in such a way as to make the connection clear enough to command his attention.

Since the book was last revised much more systematic knowledge of the activities of managers has become available, and more analysis of the competences and qualities required for effective management (Mintzberg, 1973; Boyatzis, 1982). This enables a good deal more to be said about the actual and potential contribution of the social sciences to management than was possible a few years ago.

In 1951 Sune Carlson, a Swedish social scientist, decided to observe and record carefully and in detail the activities of a small number of senior managers. There followed a number of similar investigations (e.g. Stewart, 1967; Marples, 1967; Horne and Lupton, 1965) which used several techniques, including self-recording by managers themselves. Mintzberg collated the results of this work and of his own inquiries and was able to draw some general conclusions about the nature of managerial work, and the implications for the training and development of managers. Boyatzis was also interested in the activities of managers but his emphasis was on discovering which competences managers needed if they were to perform effectively, and which of these competences had the closest association with effectiveness as a manager. The results, which can now be briefly presented, show that the original idea of the book was a good one. They also suggest a slightly different emphasis and some new material. These have been included in this edition.

Mintzberg deduces from his own and others' observations of managerial work that the manager typically has ten working roles – three interpersonal roles, three informational roles, and four decisional roles, listed as follows:

Interpersonal	Figurehead
	Leader
	Liaison man
Informational	Monitor
	Disseminator
	Spokesman
Decisional	Entrepreneur
	Disturbance handler
	Resource allocator
	Negotiator

These roles have a different emphasis from one manager's job to another and Mintzberg's observations suggest that there are eight managerial job types, each of which emphasizes one or more of the roles. For example, a manager whose job brings him into contact with managers from other organizations emphasizes the liaison and figurehead roles, whereas a manager who has to get results from a complex manufacturing facility finds disturbance-handling a main activity. The specialist – e.g. a manager of research and development – finds he is more of a monitor and spokesman. It is possible, using Mintzberg's ideas, for an observer to analyse the activities of any manager's job to discover to what extent the ten roles are emphasized. My colleagues and I have devised a simple method which can be used by the manager himself. The manager lists the activities that fill his hours and days and estimates the time he spends on each of them. He then uses the ten Mintzberg roles to classify the activities. He can then see how much time he spends in each role and ask questions about whether, if he is to improve his performance, he ought to change his pattern of activities. As an example, the table below was completed by the director of a large teaching and research unit of a university. The difference

Eating working lunches, etc.	2					2					4
External lecturing			1			1					2
Internal lecturing			1	1			1				10
Travelling				1	10	1					2
Visiting organizations			1	1	1		1		1	1	2
Planned meetings – staff		1	1					1			3
Planned meetings – students								1			2
Meetings – university	2	2	2		1					1	10
Reading books/articles				2					1		2
Writing books/articles					4		2				2
Actual job content %	5	5	16	17	21	17	2	13	3	1	100
Ideal job content %	10	10	14	10	10	16	10	4	10	6	100
Difference	-5	-5	+2	+7	+11	+1	-8	+11	-7	-5	4

Table 1 A method of self-recording and evaluation of management activities

Activities	Figurehead	Leader	Liaison	Monitor	Disseminator	Spokesman	Entrepreneur	Disturbance handler	Resource allocator	Negotiator	Time Taken %
Meetings – outside	1		1								2
Meetings – inside											6
Paperwork – at desk											10
Writing internal documents		2	2	2	2	2		2	2		6
Reading internal documents			2	4	2	2		2			6
Writing external documents			4	4		6					10
Reading external documents				4							8
Receiving visitors			2			4					4
Random contacts – visitors											4
Random contacts – staff								4			4
Random contacts – students								3			3

Mintzberg Roles

column is a measure of the extent to which he judges his actual activity pattern against the activity pattern he believes would make him more effective.

Mintzberg suggests that a further element in this process of self-study might be for the manager to ask himself questions which will help him improve his performance in the various roles he has identified. Some of those questions are so very relevant to the relationship between management and the social sciences that they are worth citing.

Do I have powerful enough mental models of those things in the organization that I must understand? How can I develop more effective models?

What rate of change am I asking my organization to tolerate? Have we sufficiently analysed the impact of this change on the future of the organization?

Are we experiencing too many disturbances? If so, why?

How do subordinates react to my management style? Am I sufficiently sensitive to their reactions?

Do we have problems of coordination because subordinates make too many decisions independently?

These are all questions relating to a manager's understanding of the context in which he works. There are many examples from the work of social scientists which illuminate these and other questions posed by Mintzberg.

Boyatzis's work differs from Mintzberg's in that it concentrates on the relationship between managerial competences and managerial performance in the expectation that, if sufficient were known about that relationship, it would indicate what ought to be included in management education and development, and with what emphasis.

For our purposes the utility of Boyatzis's study is that it helps define which ideas and skills, derived from social science, could possibly be relevant to the successful performance of the manager's job. His findings are therefore summarized briefly in order to underline the justification for social science. They enable us to move away from the very general assumptions that were the original *raison d'être* of this book. These were that the analyses and findings of social scientists about the behaviour of people in organizations must by definition be useful to managers; useful in the sense of making them better, in some vague sense, as managers.

We can now start to be a little more precise – at least to the extent that British managers are similar to the managers from the USA who made up the sample studied by Boyatzis.

Some of those managers were described as superior performers, others as average performers. There was a third category of poor performers. The criteria used to assign managers to the three categories included objective records of performance and the opinions of senior and subordinate colleagues. Having categorized managers in this way, the next step was to list some managerial competences and to measure them. This made it possible to establish the extent to which the possession of certain competences was associated with superior performance. The competences were clustered under the six headings given below. Brief definitions are given beside each one.

1. *Goal and action*:

efficiency orientation	a concern to do something better
pro-activity	a disposition to take action to accomplish something
diagnostic use of concepts	ways of thinking which identify patterns in an assortment of information
concern with impact	i.e. with symbols of the power to have impact on others

2. *Leadership*:

self-confidence	knowing what one is doing and feeling that one is doing it well
use of oral presentations	effective verbal communication regardless of size of audience
logical thought	placing events in causal sequence
conceptualization	recognizing structure in the facts

3. *Human resource management*:

use of socialized power	using influence to build teams, networks, etc.
positive regard	positively believing in the goodness of people

23

| management of group processes | stimulating others to work effectively in group settings |
| accurate self-assessment | having a realistic view of oneself |

4. *Directing subordinates*;

development of others	coaching, helping subordinates to do the job
use of unilateral power	using forms of influence to ensure compliance
spontaneity	expressing oneself freely or easily

5. *Focus on others*:

self-control	inhibiting personal needs in the service of organization needs
perceptual objectivity	being little affected by bias and prejudice
stamina and adaptability	toughness, flexibility (physical and mental)
concern with close relationships	caring about building interpersonal relationships

6. *Specialized knowledge*:

relevant knowledge, or knowledge used	knowing what should be known for thinking and for doing
function, product, or technology focus	knowledge of a specialism
memory	accurate, appropriate and rapid recall of events and information

Boyatzis's work shows that not all the competences are equally and closely connected with effective performance for all levels and types of managers. However, there is ample evidence that there are many competences having to do with, for example, understanding organizations, handling people and diagnosing problems, for which social science knowledge would be extremely useful – not to say essential – for the effective performance of most managerial jobs.

2

Early Contributions to the Theory of Organization and Management

The intellectual origins of the contemporary social science of organization are many. From the beginning of organized social life man has theorized, speculated and moralized about the relations of the individual in and to society. Yet it would be fair, I believe, to trace the origins of the systematic study of *industrial* organizations to Taylor (1947) and other scientific managers such as Gantt and Gilbreth. These men were not professional philosophers, or social scientists. They were intelligent and energetic practical managers, driven by the problems of their time to a preoccupation with the relationship between the individual and the organization of the enterprise in which he worked. At the end of the nineteenth century, when Taylor began to practise and to write about his ideas, the problem of achieving efficiency in large, technically complex factories was a relatively new one. He considered that the main obstacle to efficiency was a failure by managers to find ways to coordinate and control the work of operatives while at the same time offering rewards for their cooperation which would satisfy them. Specifically, he claimed that managers had not systematically studied the work of operators in order to find better methods of working, but had left that to the operators, with disastrous results for efficiency; nor had managers paid sufficient attention to the control of the work of operators by personal supervision and various incentives. He himself set out to devise methods of job study, control of work flow and incentives, and he succeeded brilliantly.

It is not necessary in a book written for managers by a social scientist to describe the technical achievements of scientific management. They are to be seen in time and motion study, systems of payment by results, production control systems, and so on. What is of interest here is the theory about the organization and the individual which is implicit in Taylor's techniques.

Taylor could discern no reason beyond bad management for

conflict between the worker on the one hand and the owners and the managers on the other. It was evident to him that the prosperity of the working man was tied to the prosperity of the firm. Therefore, any steps to improve that prosperity, such as the methods of scientific management, would be welcomed once it was explained that this *was* the objective, and that the individual worker would benefit. He, the worker, would also accept the division of the task in which the managers and the technical specialists were the organizers and the controllers, and the industrial operators the 'doers', because he would see this, as Taylor himself did, as a prerequisite of efficiency. Therefore, the movement to end rule-of-thumb management, which was Taylor's life's work, was regarded by him not only as a contribution to industrial efficiency but also as a specific remedy for industrial strife and management–worker conflict in all its forms.

The philosophy which, more than any other, still influences the behaviour of managers in pursuit of efficiency in modern manufacturing organization is that of 'scientific management'. This is so despite the many theoretical, moral and practical objections that have been raised against it, and which will be referred to presently.

As engineers concerned with a problem of the organization of manual workers, the scientific managers stressed the significance of physical activities. For them, the industrial worker was a kind of mechanism who would, if he were given the right rewards, submit to being set up to produce, in pre-determined ways, certain defined bits of work. This summary, although in its essentials fair, is however too crude adequately to represent Taylor's thought. He and the other scientific managers always stressed the importance of getting the right atmosphere, of taking account of the attitudes of workers, and of the necessity to explain. But the procedures for getting the right atmosphere were never worked out systematically. The theoretical framework of scientific management, with its crude psychology and sociology, was inadequate for this task.

When Taylor and his colleagues observed behaviour which was not prescribed by the organization as formally necessary to achieve its objectives, their attitude was to condemn rather than to explain. For example, the practice of groups of workers setting ceilings on output, below the targets set by managers, was to Taylor an evil. He regarded 'systematic soldiering', as he called it, as an understandable reaction to a lack of proper control by management, and the working man was therefore not to be individually condemned for it. But it benefited nobody, it was demoralizing, and so it was an evil. Taylor's ideas of human motivation were primitive, and he never understood the significance of groups in organizations. Organizations were seen as disorderly aggregates of individual human beings drilled into formal order and given direction by formal structure and procedures of planning and control instituted by management.

All these criticisms of scientific management have the benefit of hindsight. Contemporaries of Taylor who criticized his methods, and there were many, mostly did so on the humanitarian ground that speed-up was a bad thing for the health and well-being of workers. There were also trade-union critics busy averting a threat to their interests and the interests of their members as they saw them. For Taylor had no use for trade unions and blamed them for encouraging restrictive practices which, he argued, were *against* the workers' interests. There is, so far as I am aware, no contemporary critique of Taylor based on a charge of theoretical inadequacy. These were to come later.

Max Weber and bureaucracy

Weber (1864–1920) was a contemporary of Taylor. This German scholar has greatly influenced modern sociology and, like Taylor, though for different reasons, he was interested in formal organization, i.e. in the rational means employed to direct the activities of many individuals with different jobs towards given objectives. Weber was a student of the history of social organization. He wrote much about the many forms of social organization found in human history and he theorized about the reasons for their emergence and decline (Weber, 1946). From our point of view it is his interest in modern bureaucracy which matters. In everyday usage bureaucracy is synonymous with red tape and inefficiency. In Weber's usage it is a type of organization. Bureaucracy will rarely be found in its pure form but it is, as it were, a prototype for an efficient modern large-scale organization. Unlike Taylor, Weber was not a passionate advocate for his theories, nor a practical administrator. He was, as a scholar, interested in what was happening in industrialized societies and in trying to find ways systematically to describe it and compare it with what was happening elsewhere and what had happened in other periods of history. From his inquiries have come ideas and ways of thinking about organizations which still influence social scientists.

What intrigued Weber about large-scale modern organizations was the method by which they perpetuated themselves. Individuals came into organizations, worked in them, left them, and the organizations continued to exist. Why? How does an organization exercise authority over the persons who for the time being are its members? In short how is it managed? He distinguished three elements which together constitute what he called bureaucratic authority:

1. Fixed official duties.
2. Rules about authority and coercion.
3. Methodical provision for the fulfilment of duties and the exercise of rights.

To take these in order: bureaucracies are distinguished by the methodical way they distribute and define official duties. That is to say they define certain areas of competence. In managerial parlance, care is taken about job descriptions throughout the organization and the way the jobs interrelate. Now official duties carry responsibilities for getting things done. To get things done necessitates having authority to impose sanctions and to distribute rewards. But this power must be limited by the rules which govern the office. It must not be arbitrary. There is in a bureaucracy a special concern to see that a person is competent to fulfil the duties and obligations required by the office. Therefore, selection and training for office, done systematically, must be a feature of bureaucracy. Since bureaucracies have hierarchical, pyramid-shaped, social structures, with greater authority and heavier responsibility at the top than at the bottom, they tend to provide for continuity at the top by recruitment from the layers below. The prospect of promotion acts as a spur to organizational loyalty and ensures efficient successors at every level, provided that careful selection and training is devised to that end and proper qualifications specified.

A bureaucracy also ensures permanence by the keeping of files and records, i.e. the know-how remains in the organization and does not pass out with individuals who leave. It tends to separate the organizational life of the incumbent of office from his private life and to imbue him with ideas of service to the organization as a profession or vocation.

The nearest thing to Weber's notion of bureaucracy is the civil service, but it is not difficult to see in his description features of large-scale organizations in manufacturing and commerce and perhaps some small ones. It is not difficult either to see that in a sense Taylor and the scientific managers exemplified the processes of bureaucratization that Weber described. They were certainly interested in defining areas of competence, in distributing authority and in methodical provision for the performance of duties and the exercise of rights. They were mainly interested, however, in the organization of manual work. Discussion of the theory and practice of bureaucratic *management* is to be found in the writings of those whom I have chosen to describe as *the theorists of formal organization*. The work of these writers, particularly Fayol and Urwick, will be described presently.

In Taylor's time psychologists had not yet shown much interest in the problems of the individual in an organizational context, although there were isolated exceptions. The problems of industrial organization in the First World War stimulated the application of psychological knowledge to industry and gave birth to *industrial psychology*.

The British industrial psychologists

The problem of creating organizations which are efficient and which at the same time satisfy the desires, aspirations and interests of those who work in them has attracted workers from all the social sciences, as well as practical administrators. Max Weber saw the problem largely as one of constructing a rational system of authority for the efficient pursuit of defined objectives. He was therefore concerned more with problems of social structure than with the psychological problems of adjusting persons to roles. He was probably inclined to assume that this could be taken care of by careful role definition, by selection and training and by a rational system of rewards and punishments in the organizations. In many respects Taylor took the same position, although he was greatly concerned with the details of systems of rewards and punishments for industrial workers. Industrial psychologists placed the emphasis much more on the problems of the individual in carrying out his organizational role than on the design of the organization. One reason for this was the tradition of the psychology of their time, which was interested especially in explaining and measuring the differences

29

between individuals. Another was the type of problem confronting the psychologists.

The first industrial researches of any consequences by psychologists were done in England in the First World War under the auspices of the Health of Munition Workers Committee and its successor the Industrial Fatigue Research Board. The scarcity of labour, the large influx of women into industry and the insatiable demand for munitions defined the problems to be studied. How many hours a day can a man, or woman, go on working and still come each morning fit for each new day's work? What effect do poor lighting and ventilation have on the level of output of industrial workers? Are there any ways of improving the methods of work so that output improves and at the same time the work is made easier, less boring, more satisfying? These problems demanded that existing knowledge of physical and mental fatigue had to be applied and new knowledge gained. There were also the problems of the proper selection and training of industrial workers to be investigated and new systems to be devised.

So useful was this work that it was carried on after the war (Myers, 1933). Although a wider range of problems is now studied, the tradition is continued to this day by the Industrial Psychology Unit of the Medical Research Council. The National Institute of Industrial Psychology, a private foundation established in 1921, does much the same range of research work. Its main support comes from industry and it has a very practical bent. At its inception there was some suspicion that it was practising Taylorism under another name, whereupon it was explained that the work of the NIIP was based upon sound psychology rather than on a mechanical analogue of the human being. It sought not to push the worker from behind but to ease his difficulties, and by this means to increase his output and his personal satisfaction. In recent years, as psychological knowledge has grown, psychologists have increased the range of their research and consulting work, but they are still very much concerned with physical working conditions, selection procedures and the like.

Although the British psychologists were right to say that they were not Taylorists, they were, like Taylor, interested in finding ways to improve the productive performance of industrial workers, while at the same time keeping the workers healthy and satisfied. They differed in that the psychologists had a much more refined conception of the complexities of the individual human organism and were interested in the further refinement of that conception. Like Taylor, they also emphasized the physical rather than the social (organizational) environment, although they showed an awareness of the positive influence of the latter which was lost on Taylor.

The differences and the similarities between Taylor and the early industrial psychologists are illustrated by their approach to the subject of rest pauses for manual workers. Both were interested in so arranging spells of work and rest that output would be maximized. The rapid onset of fatigue after long spells of work was to be avoided by judiciously spaced rest periods. In this way the worker would go home healthily tired at the end of the day having done a good day's work. But Taylor had a crude common-sense theory about fatigue, a lack of appreciation of the influence of sentiment in human working relationships, and homespun ideas of motivation. Nor, for all his commitment to science, did he seem to be aware of a need to improve on common sense in explaining human behaviour. The industrial psychologists were aware of this need and worked with admittedly imperfect but tested knowledge about, for example, human muscular fatigue, human motivation and human instincts and emotions.

The work of the industrial psychologist in the past fifty years has had its impact on industry. Much is now known and applied about selection procedures, about methods of training and about fatigue; and the psychologists have contributed greatly to the design of machines and buildings, so that these are more appropriate to the needs of the working human being. The modern science of ergonomics which studies the relationship between man and machine is a specialized branch of industrial psychology. It also borrows much from engineering. Ergonomics is a science with an intensely practical bent, being concerned with finding ways of designing the machine and the relation of the man with it that will result in greater machine efficiency *and* human satisfaction with work.

It is not my intention here to attempt to describe in detail the findings of the industrial psychologists, or even to summarize them. But they play an important part in the story of social science and industry.

One of the early homes of industrial psychology was Harvard University. From its Graduate School of Business, and from Elton Mayo in particular, came the idea for the researches at the Hawthorne works of the Western Electric Company near Chicago.

These experiments, which began in the tradition of British industrial psychology, were to have a marked effect on the development of the application of social science to industry, and on the practice of management.

Elton Mayo and the Hawthorne experiments

It is as well to begin a brief account of the Hawthorne experiments with a reminder that the problem being studied was the same general problem as had faced all the other inquirers whose work we have discussed, namely what are the factors in the physical and social environment of the person working in an organization which affect his working performance and his personal satisfaction with his work? Like the British industrial psychologists, the Hawthorne researchers had a strong applied bent – they wanted to use their findings to improve output and satisfaction at the Hawthorne plant, as well as to add to the stock of knowledge in social science.

In November 1924 some experiments on the effect on output of lighting of various intensities were started. These were carried out in actual working departments and the results showed no positive relation between the two variables. It was therefore assumed that the experimental design was faulty and that better isolation and control of the variables should be attempted. A test group and a control group were formed. The surprising result was a similar and appreciable increase of output *in both groups*. The experimenters were puzzled but persistent. Their further efforts, however, only led them inexorably to the conclusion that it was impossible to isolate and measure one or two variables when studying a natural work group. They therefore decided to set up experimental groups in which it would be easier to isolate and measure the variables, and for their first study with such groups they chose the problem of rest pauses and fatigue. These were problems with which, as we saw, the industrial psychologists and Taylor had been greatly concerned. The Hawthorne investigators were sure that their own experiences with the lighting experiments cast doubt on the methods by which existing knowledge of rest pauses and fatigue had been gained; they set out to remedy this by careful experimental design.

But the results of subsequent experiments left the experimenters a little puzzled. After all their carefully controlled changes in hours of work, rest pauses and so on, they were unable to halt a general upward trend in the rate of output. Even a lengthening of the working day and a reduction of rest pauses seemed to have little or no depressing effect. The general upward trend, despite changes, was astonishing (Roethlisberger and Dickson, 1939, page 86).

The problem raised set the investigators planning further experiments to test the effects of changes in methods of wage payment on output, or of changes in the supervisor–worker relationship; effects which it was suspected had intervened adventitiously to influence earlier experiments. The experimenters were led a step further to the conclusion that every factor in a work situation is so closely related to all the others that any attempt to hold one constant will change the others.

For example – and I quote the researchers' own words –

The efficiency of a wage incentive was so dependent on its relation to other factors that it was impossible to consider it as a thing in itself having an independent effect on the individual (page 160).

The management of the factory began to see that

such factors as hours of work and wage incentives were not things in themselves having an independent effect upon employees' efficiency; rather, these factors were no more than parts of a total situation and their effects could not be predicted apart from that total situation (page 185).

Now the methods of the investigators changed. They were looking at the organization and its constituent departments as a social system and not as aggregations of individuals who were passive recipients of pushes and pulls in the direction of increased efficiency. But not only did their methods change – the break with tradition was more remarkable in that they began to give importance not to lighting, ventilation, rest pauses, selection and so on, but to attitudes, to social relationships at work, and to supervisory behaviour. In short they were moving nearer to a theory which took account of the characteristics of the individual and the way these influenced, and were influenced by, relationships in the organization. The researchers concluded that attention should be directed to the definition of the role of the supervisor and his selection and training, because his behaviour was a major influence on morale. They also recommended a programme of confidential interviews to give workers an opportunity to complain, to suggest or simply to let off steam.

The Hawthorne experiments suggested that interferences with the equilibrium between the individual and the social reality around him were not due, at any rate in the Hawthorne works, to physical conditions, i.e. they did not arise from fatigue, monotony, boredom, etc. Nor were they due to neurosis, i.e. to failures in the mental capacity of individuals to adjust to reality. These interferences arose out of the social relations of the individual both outside the factory and on the job.

In their famous later observations in the Bank Wiring Room, the investigators studied the process by which a group of workers controlled the pace of work and the system of wage payment so as to produce results satisfactory to it *as a group* but unsatisfactory to management. They concluded, as against Taylor, that this kind of behaviour is not just the result of bad management – in the technical sense of controlling output and earnings – but the outcome of the group protecting itself *as a group* from what it perceives to be a hostile environment, i.e. the organization as a whole, or at least those members of it with whom they have close contact, the supervisor, the time-study man and so on.

As a result of the popularization of the Hawthorne experiments, it is certain that managers have been influenced indirectly, perhaps unknowingly, by their results. They have been influenced even more, and more directly, by the writings of the theorists of formal organization. The ideas of Fayol in France, Mooney and Reilly in America and Urwick in Britain have gained widespread acceptance amongst managers, probably because their work was primarily directed towards the practical improvement of management. In so far as they were interested in theories of organization, it was to assist in this general improvement. Although they have much in common with Weber, these writers seem to have been entirely unaware of his work. Like Taylor, they were practical men interested in the problems of their time, problems of large-scale organizations with complicated technologies. They were also interested to see how far the experience of large-scale organizations like armies was of relevance to the problems of industrial organization.

Theorists of formal organization: Fayol and Urwick

In the writings of Fayol and Urwick there are two interwoven strands which are very difficult to disentangle. One is the attempt at an abstract description of the elements of formal organization,*

* This term refers to those elements of organization which relate directly to organizational purposes and objectives and are designed to do so.

the other a set of practical guides to action in the design and management of organizations. The method of exposition these writers employed was to draw upon their own practical experience and that of others to define the salient features of efficient organization, and then to describe methods for the design and management of efficient organizations and some of the problems to be solved in the process.

Organizations exist for purposes, say Urwick (1934) and Fayol (1949); they have objectives. Efficient organizations are precise in defining their objectives; they are also careful to look ahead to discern likely future happenings which will demand a reformulation of objectives. Organizations must decide what activities have to be carried out to fulfil the objectives, and to assign these activities to persons. However, efficient organizations are careful not to define activities or to assign them by reference to particular individual persons. They define tasks impersonally, taking into account the relation between the tasks and the problem of their coordination without reference to any existing persons. Having done so, they then think about the persons and the problems of fitting them to the jobs and relating them to other persons in other jobs. In short, they define the formal organization of jobs, and then try to fit people as closely as possible to them. It will never be a perfect fit, so the argument goes, human nature in general being what it is and individuals differing so much from one another.

There are in formal organizations, according to these theorists, problems of the distribution of authority, authority being defined as the power to require other persons to do things. There are also problems of equating authority with responsibility. That is to say, a person in a job must know what activities and resources of the organization and of other persons in it he is to be held accountable for and to whom; and he must be given power to get done those things for which he is held accountable. If he has less authority than responsibility he will not get things done efficiently. If he has more, then it is either redundant or dangerous or both, and certainly inefficient. Theorists of formal organization insist that power be distributed rationally in organizations, i.e. in the service of objectives. This must always be borne in mind when tasks are being assigned. Individuals must have no more power than is necessary for the efficient discharge of their duties.

Organizations, the formal organization theorists go on to say, employ specialists, persons who are 'authorities on' rather than having 'authority over'. Problems arise as to what ought to be the relationship between the 'authorities over' and the specialist. The efficient solution to this problem is to put the 'authorities over' into a chain of command, in which the areas of responsibility and the corresponding spread of authority diminish as one comes down the organization from the chief executive. The 'authorities on', the functional specialists, are not in this chain of command but are there to provide a technical service to it. If a technical function becomes a largish organization itself, as, for example, a design and development section, or a work study department, then it might have its own internal chain of command. On no account, however, must the authority within the specialist sub-organization cut across the main chain of command. This only leads to confusion and inefficiency.

One problem of the practical design of organizations is to decide how many persons one other person can effectively have under his authority, or, to put it the other way, how many can he efficiently be held responsible for – the problem of the span of control. This is really a part of the general problem of job or activity assignment. It has to do with coordination, and its corollary the problem of information flow. If one looks at the experience of large formal organizations with long chains of commands, such as armies and large industrial units, one finds, say the theorists of formal organization, that they are careful to have about six, certainly not more than ten, people answering to any one person. Therefore, one ought to follow what has been found empirically to work and to construct one's organization accordingly.

Findings of research by Koontz, an adherent of the theory of formal organization, suggest that the appropriate span of control could vary widely from situation to situation, even within a single organization. For example, if those being managed work in close proximity doing similar and simple jobs then a wider span of control would be appropriate than if the opposite set of conditions obtained. Having identified in his research the factors that affect the span of control, Koontz has proposed a numerical method for determining the appropriate span given the circumstances of a particular case. Aspects of this work help bridge a gap that exists between the theory of formal organization and the radical departures from that theory that are discussed later in this book (Koontz, 1966).

The difficulty of disentangling theory from exhortation in the work of the theorists of formal organization is nowhere more marked than in the discussion of leadership and delegation, and its relation to the span of control. Leadership, if I have understood these writers, is to them a principle of organization. One would have thought it to be an attribute of persons, or a generalized description of a certain type of social behaviour. The organizational process which, we are told, accompanies the principle of leadership is the process of delegation. There is a temptation for a man in authority to take on too much responsibility himself. It is much more efficient to encourage in subordinates a sense of responsibility and this can only be done if they are assigned work, allowed to get on with it, and made accountable for it. Put like this, it would seem that the process of task assignment is something which becomes the prerogative of particular superiors in their search for organizational efficiency. The actual division of labour in an organization and the shape of the pyramid of command would, on this view, be the outcome of numerous personal decisions to delegate. Yet another view of the same assignment problem is that the tasks are allocated not by personal decision but in relation to objectives, and according to a master organizational plan. It may be that in a given organization both these processes go on.

Urwick, in his book *The Elements of Administration*, says that he is using an engineering analogy in his analysis of organizations because men are not sophisticated enough yet to understand and work with an organic one. It is useful, he says, to think about organization as a problem of design. And to some extent he discusses organizations in terms of questions like: What is an organization for? How does one put an organization together? How does one keep it running? But all the way through the discussion of problems of leadership, coordination and control, the inadequacy of the engineering model shows up. Not until recent years have sociologists and social psychologists shown the value of working consciously with an organic analogy. The work of the Hawthorne investigators was an important step in that direction, but it had little influence on theories of formal organization. In their theoretical ideas, the formal organization theorists were closer to Weber than to Mayo. Their efficient organization is closely akin to a Weberian bureaucracy. Because of their practical bias they also raise, as Weber does not, many of the problems which arise for managers in the creation and in the maintenance of organizations. The theorists of formal organization do not, however, integrate these practical insights into their theoretical model very well. They are very interested in the question of the relationship of the individual, particularly the individual manager, to the organization, yet they make little use of the work of social psychologists and sociologists. They often discuss management very much in terms of practical flair; a business of using good judgement, picking up practical hints and so on. They do not seem to hold out much hope of the possibility that human behaviour in organizations might yield to systematic analysis and be susceptible to theoretical treatment. If human behaviour is problematical, this, they hint, is because of the effect of personal idiosyncrasy on formal organization.

The formal organization theorists, and Weber, have also been criticized for only having raised problems of organization without having proposed solutions to them. It is said, for example, that although we are told that there are problems about the best way to assign and coordinate tasks so that the ends of the organization are served, and although the nature of these problems has been well defined, we are nowhere told just how these problems are to be solved in any given situation. One aspect of the assignment problem, which is also frequently raised, is whether and in what circumstances it is better to organize by process division or by product division. No answer is given to this one either, say the critics, only vague general practical hints to managers. The critics may well be right; yet it may still be claimed that Fayol, Urwick and others of the same school did a great service by identifying and stating clearly many problems in the design of formal organizations. They also indicated to managers, and commented wisely upon, the problems of authority, responsibility, leadership, delegation and so on, which arise in the day-to-day running of an organization.

The emerging social science of organization

So far, in this discussion of the development of ideas of the nature of human organization for work, we have considered the contributions made by a group of social scientists with an interest in the practical problems of organization and management – the industrial psychologists and the Hawthorne investigators; and those made by a group of practical administrators interested in systematically presenting and theorizing about the problems of organization and management – Taylor and the scientific managers, and the theorists of formal organization. We also examined briefly some of Weber's ideas about the nature of modern bureaucracy. We are still left with many unanswered questions. Some attempts to answer these questions are described later in more detail. Here they are summarized briefly.

Some of the problems of the individual in relation to the organization were investigated by the Hawthorne researchers and the industrial psychologists. Theoretical developments in psychology now make it possible to speak with greater confidence about the nature of the human organism; and as we come to know more about the nature of organizations it is possible to say more about how the human organisms might be affected by organizational procedures and controls. It is therefore possible now to suggest patterns of organization and management which will release individual potential. Amongst the chief contributors to the development of theories about the relation between the organization and the individual are Likert (1967), Argyris (1957) and McGregor (1960). Their ideas are based on carefully planned and executed research into the structure and functioning of organizations and the behaviour of individuals and groups within them. However, this work does not lack its critics and these will be mentioned in a later chapter. The University of Michigan group under Likert has also researched into the relationship between supervisory style, productivity and the morale of working groups.

A neglected factor in the work we have so far discussed is technology. The industrial psychologists did concern themselves with problems of fatigue and boredom arising from repetitive work and the effect of this on output, but the effects of changes in technology on organizations and on the satisfaction and well-being of the people in them have until quite recently been relatively neglected. For example, the principles of organization and management proposed by the theorists of formal organization claimed universal applicability, regardless of the particular organizational setting in which they were applied. Weber's ideal-type bureaucracy was also a kind of prototype for an efficient, modern large-scale organization – governmental, industrial or commercial. Yet, now that it has been pointed out, it does not seem difficult to see that forms of organization appropriate to one purpose might be quite inappropriate to another, or that technology, i.e. the technical procedures and equipment available, might limit organizational alternatives, or that technology might play a large part in the process of human task definition and might place limits on human interaction and thus affect satisfaction and morale.* British researchers have played a leading role in the study of organization and technology, notably Burns and Stalker (1961), Woodward (1965) and Scott *et al*. (1956). In America, Walker and Guest (1952) have studied the impact of assembly-line technology on worker satisfaction and on patterns of supervision.

The study of social groups in industry, given impetus by the Hawthorne researches, has gone on. The University of Michigan team has worked on groups; so too have the Tavistock Institute of Human Relations and individuals in various universities in Britain and the USA, e.g. Roy (1954), Lupton (1963), Cunnison (1965), Wilson (1962) and Sayles (1958). The theoretical foundations for much of this work were laid by Lewin (1951) and Homans (1951). Deciding that enough was known about the structure and functioning of working groups to make fairly accurate prediction possible, Zaleznik, Christensen and Roethlisberger at Harvard attempted with some success to do some predicting, and they have published their results (1958).

It will have become clear that the emphasis has now shifted from armchair theorizing (Weber) and generalization from particular attempts at practical problem solving (Taylor, Fayol, etc.) to a concern with the scientific investigation of human behaviour in organizations. Since Hawthorne, most of the theoretical writing on organization and management has been done by practising social scientists from universities; not much by practising industrial managers. But in Britain the Chairman of the Glacier Metal Company, Wilfred Brown, has written much arising from his managerial experience and from the research which he subsequently encouraged in his organization first by the Tavistock Institute and then by Elliott Jaques.

Social scientists interested in the development of theory have naturally come to publish their results for an audience of social scientists rather than for an audience of managers. This has sometimes meant that the practical relevance of their results has either not been examined at all, or has been missed because of difficulties of communication, or because of a confusion about what are

* The charge that social science is the pursuit of the obvious may with justice be answered by pointing out how the obvious is so often missed by managers and social scientists alike.

problems of management and what are theoretical problems.

A good example of this is to be found in the work in the sociology of organizations which has followed from Weber. Merton, amongst others, has criticized Weber on theoretical grounds, arguing that for various reasons an organization designed along the lines of Weber's ideal-type bureaucracy would not necessarily be efficient.* Merton (1957) has argued, for example, that to define tasks and procedures in detail and to train people narrowly and intensively to perform them might render them (the people) incapable of adjusting easily to change. One of Merton's students, Gouldner, made an empirical study of an industrial firm where the process of bureaucratization was going on, and proposed, as a result, that Merton's theoretical ideas of 'bureaucratic dysfunction' were borne out by the facts of this case and that Weber's theoretical categories were too crude. He suggested how they might best be refined. A team of social scientists at Aston in England, following up theoretical leads from many disciplines, have recently worked out a scheme for making operational some of Weber's concepts,† as a basis for the comparative study of organizational structure and behaviour (Pugh *et al.*, 1963). This work will be referred to in more detail in Chapter 5.

All this theoretical interchange can be very confusing to the manager who encounters it and who is asking what appear to be simple questions about how to handle change smoothly, what kinds of incentives are best, how to deal with the conflicts that crop up in the organization, why strikes happen and how can they be prevented, whether to organize by product or process, how to deal with the specialist in the organization, and so on. But neither the questions nor the answers are as simple as they appear.

Urwick may well have been right to say that people are not yet ready to discuss organizations using organic analogues, but would rather think of them as being like machines. If this is so, they are likely to be more confused than ever by current trends in sociology and organization theory. Pursuing the general problem of finding organizational alternatives which will give a good balance of advantage between economic, technical and human satisfactions in organizations (which is after all the major problem confronting managers and from which most others derive), social scientists

---

* This criticism would also apply to the principles of the formal organization theorists.

† i.e. defining them so that they can be isolated and measured.

have been using increasingly the analogue of an organism in a changing environment. It has proved possible in this way to clarify problems of decision making – for example, choosing appropriate policies to allow the organization to remain in equilibrium with its environment, while at the same time finding the right balance of technological, economic and human satisfactions. It is also possible to make sense of some of the many problems of tension and conflict which emerge as a result of technological and administrative change. The role–personality problem makes more sense also in this framework and so does the relation of formal and informal organization. The organic model, which has shown itself a useful aid in the analysis of practical problems of managerial decision making, derives partly from social anthropology, partly from psychology. Some detailed examples of the application of this model will be presented in Chapter 5.

The theoretical and practical ideas described in this section have, by education, training and other forms of diffusion, become part of the normal modes of thought and behaviour of many practising managers. The influence of scientific management remains to this day undiminished. However, its practice has been in many instances modified by the application of knowledge about individual and group behaviour which has originated from social science research and theory. Most significant, perhaps, for both theory and practice, has been the recognition of the importance of the inter-connections between economic, technical, social and psychological variables described first by workers at the Tavistock Institute as a socio-technical system. This concept, which we shall refer to frequently, expresses the notion that all organizations, or parts of them, have a problem adapting to the economic, socio-cultural and political environment in which they happen to be. In order to adapt, they typically set themselves goals which will probably include providing goods and services in ways which economize on the use of physical and human resources. This, in turn, requires a technology (i.e. some physical and procedural means to make the goods or provide the services) and a work system comprising relations between roles and their occupants which activates the technology/procedures. As all research on human groups illustrates, these groups evolve their own processes of development and continuity. Technology can certainly influence the definition of work roles and set the scene for group development but will rarely entirely determine it, while individual and group processes can determine whether technology operates efficiently or not. Technology and organization are mutually dependent. The results of that interdependence in particular cases could lead to inefficient use of resources. The idea is very crisply set out by the late Kenneth Rice, one of the original Tavistock group.

Any production system requires both a technical organization – equipment and process layout – and a work organization relating to each other those who carry out the necessary tasks. The technological demands place limits on the type of work organization possible but a work organization has social and psychological properties of its own that are independent of technology . . . a socio-technical system must . . . have economic validity. It has in fact social, technological and economic dimensions which are interdependent but all of which have independent values of their own (Rice, 1958).

Consciously or not, this idea has influenced much of the work of the contemporary social science of organizations, as the next chapter will show.

3

Testing the Theory:
Some Individual Studies

The social scientist in industry works at his job of adding to knowledge in his subject using much the same approach as the physical scientist. He knows that many people have attempted to explain the causes and consequences of human behaviour in industry; some by trying to generalize from practical experience, others by systematic research, yet others by armchair theorizing; and he gets to know this work well. He takes some of the explanations which have been proposed, subjects them to logical criticism, and puts them in a form in which they can be tested against facts about human behaviour in organizations systematically observed. He then observes and tests. His contribution to practical affairs is measured by the extent to which, as a result of his work, it becomes possible more accurately to explain and predict the outcome of particular human activities in industrial organizations.

A study of industrial bureaucracy

It will be recalled that Weber and the theorists of formal organization held that efficiency was largely the outcome of careful attention to formal organization. Their ideas can easily be formulated as 'if . . . then . . .' statements. *If* you have clear rules and roles, systematic procedures for selection, training and promotion, the right span of control, etc., etc., *then* you will be making the best use of the resources which are available to you, in pursuit of the ends you desire. This is a fairly widely held belief amongst managers, although it is often qualified by statements about the frailty and human cussedness which interfere with the rational pursuit of those objectives which managers regard as desirable.

Gouldner, an American sociologist, some years ago decided to examine some of the ideas which are explicit and implicit in Weber's bureaucratic model, by reference to the facts. My purpose in summarizing his studies here is to show their bearing on the empirical truth or falsity of these propositions, and then to draw practical conclusions.

Weber said that bureaucracies were governed by impersonal rules. Gouldner points out that Weber paid little attention to the question of who makes the rules and to the process by which they are made. Common experience suggests that this is an important question in organizations. Whether the rules which govern behaviour are arbitrarily imposed or jointly agreed might have a great deal to do with efficiency. If it seems odd that Weber chose to ignore an obviously important question it should be remembered that he drew his examples mainly from the civil service. The relation between participation in the rules set up to govern behaviour, industrial behaviour itself, and efficiency, is one which people in industry have strong views about. It is surely useful then to examine this relationship in the light of the facts and try to get nearer the truth. This is Gouldner's method. Gouldner also noticed that Weber had skated over questions about the ends served by particular rules and their usefulness as seen by different persons and groups in an organization. There might well be conflict about goals and the rules and procedures designed to serve them. As Gouldner argues, Weber seems to be interested in structure almost to the exclusion of social process. The concept of bureaucracy is a static concept. It is pertinent to ask what factors contribute to the persistence or otherwise of bureaucratic forms. There seems to be ground for doubt whether organizations which are bureaucratic in form are necessarily efficient. It might, therefore, be begging the question to say that they survive in that form because they are efficient. The social and political pressure towards bureaucratic forms and their maintenance may not arise exclusively from a desire for technical efficiency, but for other reasons. It was with such questions in mind that Gouldner embarked upon his study of a gypsum factory in the USA.

It would be tedious to repeat arguments of social scientists about the scientific value of studies of particular cases, but a brief word is necessary on this. There is substance in the criticism which points to the dangers of generalizing from the facts of a single case, but at this stage in the development of organizational sociology there is much to be said for the study of single cases. In trying to identify significant variables it is useful to get close to the data, to know one organization well. Then if it appears possible to isolate and measure particular variables and to propose hypotheses about the relations between them, it might be worth embarking upon wider comparative studies. Gouldner studied with his colleagues one small factory of 225 people off and on for about three years. The plant was in a small semi-rural community where kinship still meant a great deal and where relationships in the community tended to be carried over into the plant, and vice versa. The men employed at the factory were parochial in their attitudes and loyalties. They distrusted the head-office people and the union organizers from the big city. This shared distrust of outside agencies helped cement relationships in the plant. Relations between managers, supervisors and workers were in consequence personal, informal, governed much more by custom and practice than by formal rule.

Even before the study began this pattern was beginning to break up. Head office, faced with more tightly competitive markets, was beginning to ask questions about the efficiency of the plant and what might be done to improve it. In two books reporting his research (1955a, 1955b) Gouldner describes the process of bureaucratization, its causes and consequences. The situation as he found it before head office moved in to tighten things up was summed up by the term 'indulgency pattern'. The workers who were interviewed were unanimous in saying that the management and the supervisors were not strict. There was a good deal of informal job changing, a blind eye was turned to certain kinds of pilfering, selection of workers for jobs was organized on the basis of friendship and kinship as much as on formal qualification. Promotion procedures operated similarly. Starting and finishing time and coffee breaks were loosely interpreted, and so on.

The workmen valued this pattern. They resented the idea that managers and supervisors should exert authority for its own sake but were conscious of a technical obligation, i.e. they were happy to accept discipline when it was seen to relate directly to production. The pattern of supervision allowed the men a great deal of control over their working environment, and this they liked. They also valued the fact that relationships within the plant were not entirely governed by the formal requirements of production, but by sentiments such as might be typical of neighbourliness or friendship in a non-industrial context.

In the previous section, the idea emerged of an organization as a socio-technical system existing in a context to which it must adapt

for the sake of survival or further development. The general characteristic of such a system is that all its parts are related to one
another in such a way that a change in one will have repercussions
on the others. If, therefore, for economic reasons, a system akin
to Weber's bureaucracy, the formal organization of Fayol and
Urwick, or the scientific management of Taylor, is introduced,
where formerly relationships were governed by custom and sanc-
tified by sentiment and tradition, then some resentment or even
opposition would not be difficult to predict, however rational those
who impose the system consider it to be.

Gouldner describes in detail the consequences of the attempted
bureaucratization of the plant by a new manager appointed by the
head office of the company with instructions to make the plant
more efficient. The new man quickly broke up the indulgency pattern. He introduced other newcomers into managerial and supervisory jobs and instituted new procedures of formal control, e.g.
work study, production control, paperwork reporting systems,
more formal procedures of selection for jobs and checks on pilfering. These measures threatened to break up the well-established
pattern of mutual rights, duties and obligations; to make things
worse, they were being imposed by outsiders. The system reacted
and the first effect was one of tension, relieved by behaviour inimical to the demands of the new regime. To counter this, the new
regime resorted to closer supervision with new supervisors. But
close supervision merely generated further tension.

The point Gouldner emphasizes is this: the new man could neither accept nor adjust to the indulgency pattern and at the same
time meet the expectations of his superiors. In any case, being an
outsider as well as a successor to the position of chief executive in
the factory, the process of adjustment would for him have taken
a long time and time was not on his side. Bureaucracy, says Gouldner, might very well be the only alternative open to a managerial
successor to control an organization in this kind of situation. Yet,
it might generate tension and resistance. Control might then only
be possible by more bureaucratic procedures, and so more tension
is generated. Therefore, it is not really helpful and practical to
advise managers, as do the theorists of formal organization and the
scientific managers, that if you want efficiency you must pay attention to formal organization. One really wants to know the likely
effects of such changes in terms of efficiency, and this in turn means
that one must understand the kind of system one is tampering with.

Without such knowledge it is impossible to predict the outcome. Nor is it wise to expect that a mere change of managerial personnel will do, because a tendency to impose bureaucratic measures seems to be inherent in the role of the successor. Again, the consequences are difficult to predict unless one has a way of analysing and describing the existing system.

In the gypsum factory the consequence of bureaucracy was a series of bitter disputes and an unofficial strike. Gouldner attributes this type of reaction not to personal ham-fistedness by the new manager, nor to bloody-mindedness and nostalgia by the workers, although these were some surface manifestations of difficulty, but rather to the attempt to disturb a stable and highly valued ongoing system of relationships. The practical conclusion to be drawn from this is that it might be wise to try to understand and to work with an existing and stable pattern of relationships if one wishes to effect change smoothly. This sounds so obvious as to be hardly worth saying; yet it is clear from Gouldner's work that there is great pressure upon a successor to a managerial role to make changes in the direction of bureaucratization and to break up customary and traditional patterns, largely because it is difficult quickly to break into them. The consequences of bureaucratization in such circumstances might well run counter to the productive efficiency which is aimed at. New job definitions, new procedures and new styles of supervision will be subjected, consciously or otherwise, to the questions: Does it fit my/our interest? Does it offend against the things I/we have come to value? Does it make me/us feel comfortable and satisfied in my/our mind? Does it seem likely to affect my/our future adversely? If the answers to these questions for an individual or a group are not satisfactory, it is useless to argue that the new system is right because it leads to productive efficiency which is what everybody wants, because this will be seen as yet another attempt to impose the kind of change which is already resented. So while it might be obvious that it is sensible to work with an existing and valued system as far as possible, one's success in doing so will rest upon one's capacity to analyse and predict. It is certainly not enough to say that attention to formal organization plus a ready tongue and human sympathy is all the equipment a manager needs. He needs some tools for the analysis of social systems. These, rather than general practical hints, are what the social scientist can best provide.

Gouldner shows, in his analysis of the gypsum factory, how useful the notion of *role expectations* can be, in explaining how human behaviour in organizations is influenced and controlled. Regularity and predictability in social relationships are highly valued by individuals. They expect that the persons they associate with, at work or in the family, will behave in predictable ways. If they do not, the individual feels tense and uncomfortable and wants to do something to make life more predictable. In all human groupings there are mechanisms for punishing people who do not behave in predictable ways and for rewarding those who do. Gradually the norms of behaviour which emerge from the desire for predictability become part of the individual's personal make-up. He sometimes does not know how to explain why he behaves regularly in the way he does. It's just 'the way we do things here'. In short, people cast other people in roles which are defined by their own expectations. These may be highly formal, as legal prescriptions and bureaucratic rules are, or they may be informal or implicit, as in custom. Because of the urge to predictability, role expectations, whether formal or informal, tend towards stable equilibrium in social systems and there is pressure for them to remain that way. This is one reason why imposed social change, say as a result of new technology, may be a difficult problem. In a later section we shall examine some of the problems of technical change from this standpoint. In the next two studies we will see the way in which technology affects role expectations and human satisfactions, and the processes by which groups attempt to control their environment to satisfy the interests and values of their members. And we shall have some new tools of analysis to introduce.

Assembly-line technology and the worker

Walker and Guest in their book *The Man on the Assembly Line* (1952) report an investigation into the factors in assembly-line work which promote satisfaction or dissatisfaction with the job. This study is in the tradition of industrial psychology but it takes full account of much of the work which has been done in social psychology and sociology since the classical studies of boredom, monotony and fatigue carried out in Britain during and after the First World War. It is concerned to trace the effects of a particular kind of production technology, the assembly line, on the attitudes of workers to their jobs.

In assembly-line technology, the pace is controlled mechanically, the work being brought to the worker and taken away on completion, usually by mechanical means. The total job of assembling a motor car, for example, is broken down minutely into repetitive tasks. Each individual task needs little skill and is easily learned. The tools and the techniques to be used are not determined or chosen by the worker but by the engineers who design the line. Typically, assembly-line jobs do not require close and continuous and deep mental attention, but neither will they perform themselves. They need, as Walker and Guest put it, 'surface mental attention'. The questions which these investigators asked were: *as seen by the worker himself*, what are the effects on job satisfaction of his immediate job, his relations with his fellow workers and the supervisors, his pay and security, his working conditions, the arrangements for promotion and transfer and relations with his trade union?

Like Gouldner's research this is a study of one case, a new and up-to-date motor car final-assembly plant in a town of more traditional industry. This situation was chosen for study because the final assembly of vehicles is the example *par excellence* of assembly-line work. In this particular case the men on the assembly line had recent experience of more traditional technologies with which to make comparison. A total of 180 workers were interviewed and their attitudes systematically recorded and analysed.

The great majority of the men interviewed in the plant had no previous experience of anything remotely resembling assembly-line work, so that they were evaluating a fairly fresh experience. However, not all of their jobs contained the same mixture of elements. Some were on a moving conveyor, others not; some were highly repetitive, others less so; the change of experience differed from man to man. However, when each worker was questioned about his job he seemed to single out the elements of mechanical pacing and repetitiveness as being particularly irksome and unsatisfying. There were exceptions. A minority positively liked mechanical pacing and its concomitants. This was also found in earlier studies, some of which are summarized in Friedmann's book *Industrial Society* (1955). The majority of workers with mechanically paced, repetitive jobs of low skill put their immediate job at the top of the list of things they disliked about their total situation in the plant, although they were highly satisfied with the pay and with the security which the job offered.

Recently published British research by Goldthorpe *et al.* (1968)

approaches the study of the behaviour of assembly-line workers from an entirely different standpoint. It suggests that people who already have an instrumental attitude to work (that is, who regard work merely as a means to an end and not a source of satisfaction in itself), are attracted by the high rewards of assembly-line work. It is not to be expected then, that they will necessarily express a liking for the work or an identity with the firm but will speak largely of good pay and security. The origins of the attitudes to work on this view are outside rather than inside the organization, in the individual's personal history, family circumstances and social class position or aspiration, for example, rather than in the structure and patterning of work. This seems plausible but it does not rule out intra-firm influences. Indeed, the relation between the extra-firm and intra-firm influences on behaviour must be one of mutual dependence. Millward, in another British study, has described an interesting example of this (1968).

None of this throws any doubt on the proposition that the technology of manufacture *to some extent* shapes the pattern of interpersonal relationships on the job. This seems obvious enough, and yet when one examines the work of the theorists of formal organization one finds scant recognition of its significance. An extreme example of this effect is the solitary individual who sits in a control room watching dials. For most of his time at work he has no interpersonal relations. In assembly-line work the effect of the design of the line on the pattern of interaction is clear. The way in which the engineers break down the job and specify the time cycle of operations and physical movements will determine the functional relationships between jobs and what opportunities will exist for conversation and other forms of social interaction. Physical conditions, such as the noise level, will set limits to the extent to which those opportunities will be utilized. In turn, all this will have its effect on the extent to which an individual feels a sense of identity with a social grouping and hence might colour his attitude to the job and to the company he works for.

In the factory studied by Walker and Guest there were some jobs which provided opportunities for social interaction where conditions, e.g. the noise level, made it possible for individuals to exploit them. The men who did these jobs perceived these social aspects of their jobs as desirable, just as those who held jobs which entailed social isolation regarded this as undesirable. When one considers that a little more than half the workers interviewed had jobs of the latter kind one is led to conclude either that it is the nature of assembly-line technology to inhibit valued social inter-action, or that it might be possible, if this element of job satisfac-tion were to enter into the calculations of the designers, so to design the jobs and layouts as to remove these inhibitions, while at the same time retaining the technical advantages of the method. Similarly, it might well be possible to look at individual jobs to see whether it is possible to make them less rigidly paced and repetitive and not lose output, by job enlargement, for example. Walker and Guest make both these points and they have been emphasized by other social scientists. However, during the 1960s and 1970s, in order to adapt to changes in product markets which called for more flexible production systems and to attract reluctant workers into the factories, engineers in Western Europe and Scandinavia began to seek alternatives to the traditional assembly line. They aimed at designs which were technically flexible, economically viable, and for the worker ergonomically and psychologically satisfying. The characteristics of this movement, which has for the moment lost its momentum, will be discussed in detail later (page 100).

Despite the existence of alternatives to the assembly line, it still remains the predominant mode for high-volume assembly of engi-neering components. We have already shown how it influences social interaction on the job. It also imposes limits on promotion opportunities and influences the relationship between the worker and his supervisor and managers. One of the objectives of assembly-line work is to reduce all jobs to a minimum skill level. This maximizes its technical and administrative advantages. Yet to the extent that uniformity of skill and payment for it are achieved, so the opportunities are limited for individuals to move from jobs of low pay, status and skill to jobs at a higher level, simply because there are no such jobs on the shop floor. The men Walker and Guest interviewed saw this as being of importance in their assess-ment of their jobs. However, in the particular plant studied there were opportunities to transfer from highly paced repetitive jobs to others less so; people liked this because their motive for wanting to move from job to job was not, on the whole, higher pay and status but escape from monotony and fatigue. Workers did not only *say* that certain elements in the job were unsatisfactory, they voted with their feet. Absenteeism and turnover were related positively to elements in the job such as machine pacing, repetitiveness and social deprivation. Satisfaction found its expression in behaviour as well as in attitude.

The view is, I think, fairly common amongst managers that good lighting and ventilation and good welfare services are important elements in job satisfaction. Possibly this view has emerged because often it is draughts and canteen food that workers officially complain about. Walker and Guest's findings on this have been amply confirmed by other investigators. They found that while good general working conditions are appreciated by workers, when looked at in relation to other factors in the job such as pay and security and machine control, they do not occupy a prominent place in job satisfaction.

Another effect of assembly-line technology is that the role of supervisors and managers is defined in a special way. Workers see a lot of the supervisors, whose job requires them to keep a constant eye on the assembly line to ensure that it keeps running continuously. They see little of the managers of the plant who are preoccupied with questions wider than the detailed technical and human coordination of shop-floor work. The workers interviewed by Walker and Guest reported that they saw a lot of their supervisors, thought that this relationship was important in job satisfaction, and on the whole were satisfied with their particular supervisors. They hardly ever saw the managers and did not regard relationships with them as important. Walker and Guest compare this with the situation in the steel industry where there is a much more frequent and important relationship with management, which seems to arise out of the imperatives of steel-making technology.

I have left Walker and Guest's findings about the place of wages and job security until last not because these are unimportant; I just wished to offset the usual exclusive concern with them by an emphasis on some other aspects of job satisfaction. I have also been anxious to establish the general importance of technology as a shaper of social structure and job definition, and to point out that variations of social structure and job definition might well be possible within the limits set by a particular technology, using the findings of *The Man on the Assembly Line* to exemplify this. In fact pay and security are of great importance in job satisfaction. A majority of workers were attracted to the assembly plant from other jobs largely because it offered much higher wages and greater security. On average, workers had gained about 50 per cent in weekly income by moving. When weighing the things they liked and disliked about the assembly-line job, 80 per cent of those interviewed placed economic factors first in their list of 'likes'. And most men also placed job security high.

It has become something of a fashion these days to question the value of trade unions to working men. Some economists argue that they are futile because they have no long-term effect on the general level of real wages. It has also been said that since employers are now becoming more aware of the economic advantages of having a satisfied labour force, there is less need for unions. Walker and Guest questioned the men on the job. Two-thirds of them were in favour of the union. It proved to be useful in handling grievances arising from the unsatisfactory elements in the job. By bringing these problems to the notice of management, improvements were initiated. The researchers concluded that membership of the union helped counterbalance the impersonality and anonymity in the job. However, the existence of a union was not seen by the men as a powerful factor affecting their like or dislike of the situation as a whole.

Walker and Guest offer us an analysis which combines the approach of the psychologist to the effects on the worker of physical conditions of work, the social psychologist who is interested in the effect on the individual of membership of a social grouping, and the sociologist whose concern is with the factors which influence the structuring of social relationships. From a slightly different standpoint their research examines some aspects of the problems which interested Gouldner, namely, the factors which influence task definition and the rules which govern relationships at work. In the case of assembly-line work, technology obviously plays a major part in bureaucratizing shop-floor relationships. It also affects the structure of management and its relations with the shop floor. Yet even assembly-line technology is not entirely limiting. Walker and Guest conclude their study by pointing to the ways in which the technology itself and the administrative arrangements for wage payment, transfer, promotion, etc., offer opportunities to management to search for alternative layouts and procedures which balance economic, technical and social satisfactions. We shall be looking more closely in a later section at subsequent attempts to exploit such opportunities in manufacturing system design and the practical difficulties that they have faced and, to some extent, overcome.

At this point it will be helpful to turn to a British study made after the Second World War which compared the influence on organizations of different production technologies. I refer to Woodward's *Industrial Organization* (1965).

The influence of production technology upon organization

In introducing Joan Woodward's work it is worth mentioning that when it appeared it threw advocates of theories of formal organization into some disarray. It will be recalled that these theories discuss the efficiency of organization mostly in terms of formal means to coordinate tasks which have been assigned as parts of a total task or objective, and they generalize about these formal means without reference to the particular tasks involved, or to the technical means employed. Studies which spread doubt by purporting to show that the technology of manufacture itself constitutes a limit on possible organization are therefore a challenge to established theory. The proponents of established theory are fighting a rearguard action. Usefully, because there are parts of their territory which are worth defending.

Woodward's avowed aim in her research was

to discover whether the principles of organization laid down by an expanding body of management theory correlate with business success when put into practice (1959, page 4).

In particular she intended to look at the relationship between line managers and specialists. It soon became clear to her that this relationship could not be studied in isolation. When comparing data collected in a hundred firms in the south-east of England it emerged that considerable variations in size, type of industry or success in business were not clearly related to patterns of organization. Yet when the firms were grouped according to similarity of objective and technology of manufacture, there did appear to be a relation between technology and organizational pattern or structure.

The firms in the sample were placed into ten different categories according to their production system. Roughly, they fell into three larger technological divisions with some slight overlap: small batch and unit production, large batch and mass production, and process production. The ten production groups form a crude scale of technical complexity, technical complexity being defined in terms of the degree of control over production and predictability of results. The general conclusion was that organizational patterns differed at different levels of technical complexity. For example, the number of levels in the managerial hierarchy increased with technical complexity. The span of control of the first line supervisor increased along the scale and reached its peak under mass production. It then declined through the process technologies. Process production seems to demand a very much higher ratio of managers to other personnel than other types of technology. Ratios of direct to indirect labour, the proportion of university graduates amongst supervisory staff, and the span of control of the chief executive all increase as one moves along the scale from low to high technical complexity. In Woodward's sample, specialization of function in management appears to be found more frequently in batch and mass-production firms. In unit-production firms there were few specialists. In process firms the line managers were also technical specialists.

Woodward also found that it was in the large-batch and mass-production firms that the actual administration of production by modern techniques of production scheduling and control, work study, and so on was the most widely separated from the personal supervision of production. Thus the solutions advanced by Taylor for production efficiency seem to be adopted efficiently over a certain range of technologies, but are not universally applicable. *Industrial Organization* indicates that one would be wise to examine every prescription for improved organization with the question in mind: Is it appropriate to this technology? This makes life much more complicated perhaps than the theorists of formal organization were ready to admit; but then life *is* complicated.

Already, having looked at the findings of Walker and Guest, we would expect technology to have its effect on job satisfaction and the quality of relationships. Woodward looks along the scale of technological complexity for evidence of changes in this respect. She finds a relation between technical complexity, as measured on her scale, and what she describes as 'the attitudes and behaviour of management and supervisory staff and the tone of industrial relations'. At both ends of the scale, pressures on people from technology seemed to be less than they were in the middle of the scale. That is to say that generally the atmosphere was more relaxed and people liked it better in one-off technologies and process technologies, than in the batch and mass-production technologies. It is worth pointing out, perhaps, that this could mean that great personal skill in leadership, delegation and so on, which is emphasized so much by the theorists of formal organization, might pay much worse dividends in efficiency and satisfaction in some technological settings than in others. This does not, of course, minimize their importance. It merely warns us not to treat them as isolated causes of efficiency or satisfaction.

The main argument of *Industrial Organization*, from the standpoint of the practising manager, is that there seems to be a pattern of organization appropriate to the technology employed. Or, to put it another way, the technology demands certain forms of organization for its efficient exploitation. In building up organizations, which can be, as the theorists of organization point out, a deliberate act of planning, one should try to be sensitive to technological demands. In her research, for example, Woodward found some firms which had consciously followed the theories of formal organization and had become inefficient in consequence because they were inappropriate technologically; successful firms which had consciously adapted organization to technology; and unsuccessful ones which had made no attempt at organization building, but which had spontaneously grown an organization pattern out of the relationships between particular influential individuals, which was inappropriate and inefficient. There is probably a fourth category, of firms which spontaneously adapt to the demands of technology and are successful.

Other studies of management and technology seem to confirm the point made in *Industrial Organization*. A study by Burns and Stalker (1961) elaborates the general point that a flexible *organic* kind of organization is most appropriate to firms in situations of rapidly changing objectives and technology, and a more formal *mechanical* kind of organization will work well where objectives and technology are well established and not subject to rapid change.

Woodward's work has been criticized because the classification of production technology is crude, and because of her excessive emphasis on one variable – technology and its relation to organization. But it makes a very useful starting point not only for a critical look at the prescriptions of formal organization theory but also for future researches, some of which we shall examine later.

It will now be interesting to ask what problems emerge when technology changes radically and quickly in the same organization.

Technical and administrative change

The resistance which is sometimes offered to the introduction of new methods of doing work in organizations, e.g. new machinery or new administrative procedures, is often thought to be due to something called 'the inherent conservatism of man'. This is to say, in effect, that the resistance is a property of human nature. Were this so, then it would not seem possible to effect changes without changing human nature. Yet we are also told that 'human nature cannot be changed'. Are we to admit, therefore, that nothing can be done? Surely not, because it is known to common sense that there are some situations of change where little in the way of resistance is encountered, and others where there is much. This seems to suggest that resistance to change might have to be explained by reference to the properties of situations rather than to the properties of individuals. But of course both are relevant. Indeed, it is hardly possible to speak of one without referring to the other.

When we were discussing Gouldner's work we saw how a disturbance of stable customary expectations, embedded as these are in existing interpersonal relationships, generates resistance to administrative changes. The individual in such situations is attempting to adapt to his social environment so as to maintain his own psychological equilibrium. In doing so he might resist what are perceived as disturbing changes – the inherent conservatism of man; but the social situation, that is his relationships with others, the social norms which govern them, and the shared interests with like folk which are associated with them, will deeply influence the way the individual interprets the change – and what he regards as disturbing. In Gouldner's factory, the workers felt that the indulgency pattern which they valued was being threatened, and from this emerged the resistance to measures of bureaucracy. Different groups, according to their particular situation, offered their own particular brands of resistance.

The reader will have discerned by now that social science theory holds that stable and customary expectations are built up from a number of ingredients. For example, the structure of relationships between persons in organizations is partly shaped by technology (Woodward, Walker and Guest, etc.) which defines the required functional interaction. It is also partly shaped by the administrative procedures which are necessary to make the technological system function and which link the organization to its external environment – to its customers, to government, and so on (Weber, Gouldner). Also, the structure may be influenced by the deliberate acts of powerful individuals, who set objectives and assign tasks. But all these influences only create as it were the bony framework of organization. They specify the jobs which need to be done, who will work with whom, for what purpose and under whose direction. The possible shape of the framework is, as we have seen, limited but not completely determined by the constraints of technology (Woodward). But the way in which the framework comes to life is through the activities of individuals in their interpersonal relationships.

We shall describe in a later section the processes by which groups form and create their own norms and sanctions to ensure conformity to those norms. For the moment it is sufficient to say that social groups form in organizations when people who work near each other, and are functionally interdependent, elaborate their relationships beyond the formal requirements of the organization. The result is sometimes referred to as the 'informal' organization, although this does not describe it well. As groups elaborate their relationships, norms and social controls, they try like individuals to get into some kind of stable equilibrium with the immediate environment, that is to say with other nearby groups, with the authority system of the organization, and so on. In some situations this process results in behaviour by the group which is inimical to the purposes of the organization as formally defined, and we have the familiar restrictive practice. In other cases this does not happen. It is of great practical importance to find some explanation for this difference. There are two British researches which have explored the problems of technological change, the Liverpool University study, *Technical Change and Industrial Relations* (Scott *et al.*, 1956), and the study from the Tavistock Institute, *Organizational Choice* (Trist *et al.*, 1963). The detailed theory of the working group which is relevant to the problems of industrial change and efficiency will be examined by reference to the work of an American sociologist, Roy (1954), and to my own book, *On the Shop Floor* (1963).

The Liverpool workers chose as their field of study a large steel plant, with what appeared to be a remarkable history of smooth assimilation to large-scale technical changes. The research was designed to analyse the impact upon the social structure of the plant of various technical changes which had taken place and others which were currently in hand. The objective was twofold, to add generally to knowledge about organizations and their problems and to try to identify in this particular case the factors which had encouraged the smooth assimilation of change. The research had a historical dimension. It was expected that the experience of previous changes and the persistence of certain patterns of relationships formed in the past, might do much to explain current behaviour in the face of change or impending change.

The plant in question manufactured sheet steel. It was the major industrial plant in a small community. When the study was undertaken in 1953 there were 7000 employees. In 1896 there had been 250 men under the personal control of the owner. The growth of the plant was accompanied by, and was partly a consequence of, both technical changes and backward integration towards the raw materials. Not only had the plant grown; the occupational composition of its working force had changed remarkably and this seemed to be largely due to the technical changes. For example, as a result of the introduction of labour-saving machinery, the percentage of direct production workers fell from 82 per cent of the working force to 65 per cent in the period from 1925 to 1953. At the same time, owing to the growing technical complexity of the processes, the percentage of people engaged in maintenance and service jobs increased more than twofold. Probably because of the administrative problems of control arising from increasing size and technical complexity, the percentage of administrative staff also doubled over the period.

The original steel-rolling process employed in the plant was the 'Staffordshire Mill', and the growth of the firm consisted in the addition of more mills, each operated by a team of ten men. This mode of expansion had no effect on occupational structure nor did it give rise to difficult managerial problems of control, because each team was largely self-contained and self-governing and was paid a wage based on the team output. In the very early years of the plant's history the leader of each team was in fact a sub-contractor to the firm. It was when the company decided to make its own steel for rolling, later to make its own iron, and then to introduce revolutionary changes in the methods of steel making and sheet rolling, that the division of labour became complicated, and management and control difficult. This had consequences for the structuring of management organization, for the type of manager required and for the patterning of shop-floor relationships. The detailed analysis of the history of the relation between technical change and social structure in this steel plant amply confirms the suspected existence of a very strong connection between technology, the structure of occupations, the formal structuring of work relations, and informal organization.

Trade unions represent the interests of various occupational groupings. In plants like this one, which had two unions sharing the organization of the process workers and fifteen unions organizing the various maintenance and service workers, there were problems arising from the impact of changing occupational structure on the spheres of influence of the unions. These problems and the methods used for their solution were also analysed in detail by the Liverpool researchers.

All these analyses confirmed the first general impression that technical change had, in fact, been assimilated without major difficulty. There had been many serious problems arising, for example, from the complete disappearance of some occupations – like the Staffordshire Mill operators – from the reduction in the proportion of men required to run the processes, from the increasing growth in the numbers and importance of the maintenance and service workers, as the plant became technically and administratively more complex. There were also problems of redundancy, transfer and retraining; problems of bonus rates, shiftwork rotas, wage differentials, trade-union demarcation and so on. Yet for all this, there was an absence of overt resistance to change, or of unmanageable conflict accompanying it. Why? What caused industrial peace in this plant? The researchers adduce several reasons for this, some of them directly related to the technology of steelmaking, others relating less directly and having to do with the administrative mechanisms for the redress of grievances and for the handling of management–worker relations. There are yet others which appear to be even less related to technological factors. These have to do with the relations between the plant and the local community.

Steel making and rolling is typically controlled by teams of operators, as for example on a Staffordshire Mill, where ten men worked in close coordination, each with his own clearly defined job, and in dirty and dangerous circumstances. The same may be said of the open-hearth steel-furnace crew or the blast-furnace crew, or even the crew of a modern strip mill, although there are differences in detail. These teams differentiate their members by function; they also arrange themselves in hierarchical order of skill and authority. Traditionally, boys are recruited from school to the lower ranks of these team hierarchies; as the years pass, they go step by step up the ladder, learning the job and accumulating seniority, until they become leading hands with high responsibility and high pay. Having once started to mount the ladder in a particular plant it is impossible for a man to transfer to another steel factory laterally. Therefore it is in his long-term interest to remain with the same company because he has a personal stake in it and in its survival. This tendency was reinforced in the plant studied (and this has been shown to be the case in other steel plants) by the mode of recruitment of young workers from the local community through the network of kinship, and by the tradition of allowing the trade union branches to adjudicate on seniority claims. Therefore there was much to generate attitudes of loyalty and identification with the company.

These considerations did not apply so strongly to the maintenance men. They do not work in functionally diversified hierarchical crews but individually or with mates or peers. For them there is no promotion by seniority. The skill of the craftsman is transferable and lateral movement is possible. The Liverpool researchers found that a much greater proportion of the craft force were immigrants to the area, they had fewer kinship ties, and their unions at national level were much less closely identified with the industry than the process-workers' unions. The craftsmen had much less of a stake in the company, and their unions less of a stake in the industry. Therefore, it was to be expected that they would take a somewhat different attitude to changes initiated by management and exploit their powerful position, which was what happened.

By contrast, the machinery for negotiation and redress of grievances, developed by the process-workers' unions and the employers, treats the shop-floor delegate as an important participant and gives him much power at shop-floor level. This machinery, which is highly valued, has helped to avoid overt conflict erupting from differences of opinion within the plant.

The informal relaxed atmosphere between manager and manager and between the workers and management seemed to have persisted in spite of the increasing size and complexity of the plant and the entry of technical specialists into management from outside. This also helped the process of assimilating change. Woodward noted in her study the way in which process technologies seem conducive to a relaxed atmosphere in industrial relations.

Steel is also an industry of low labour costs. It has, therefore, been possible for management to make concessions on wage and manning questions without adding much to the cost of the product. This has undoubtedly contributed in the past to cordial worker and union cooperation with management and has helped to get change accepted. Finally, the technology of steel-making is such that change takes a long time to implement. Plant takes years to build and this allows time to plan. Given the predisposition of managers and unions to talk, many of the problems of change can be anticipated and dealt with.

The Liverpool study shows that although the effects of technological innovation may be to change radically the social structure, it is possible, given time and appropriate machinery for the redress of grievances, to assimilate it smoothly. Because of technology and location some steel plants are particularly fortunately placed, and their traditions help. Other plants in other industries might find life less pleasant. Yet it seems clear that if they will analyse the effect of technology on their social structure, using a socio-psychological frame, they might be better able to predict the problems that change will bring and to assess whether the machinery of redress is efficient enough to cope with them, and what needs to be done to make it so. Certainly the kind of analyses which have been described in this section would be helpful.

A point is made implicitly in the Liverpool study, namely, that the efficient handling of technological change by management is a matter of finding solutions to problems which will minimize the disturbance to the existing social structure, in so far as it is already providing satisfaction, and which will maximize the economic and technical benefits of the change. *Organizational Choice* makes the point explicitly and in so doing improves upon the theoretical conceptions of the Liverpool study.

Organizational Choice is a report of researches carried out in coalmines by a group of social scientists. The approach they adopted is one they and their fellow workers at the Tavistock Institute of Human Relations had developed over a number of years. In this approach, a production system can be usefully regarded as comprising a technical organization – that is, machines and equipment deployed in given ways – and a work organization relating to the persons who perform the necessary tasks. Although the work organization is limited by the technology, it also has social and psychological properties of its own which are independent of technology. The production system comprising these two elements has also to satisfy certain economic criteria. The problem of relating organizations effectively and stably to the environments in which they operate is one of trying to balance the economic, technological and socio-psychological advantages. The hypothesis proposed is that to optimize any one of these elements does not necessarily result in a set of conditions optimal for the system as a whole. To strive for maximum technical advantage and economic reward might well create social and psychological havoc, which in turn jeopardizes economic goals. Similarly, to attempt to create high job satisfaction might adversely affect the gain to be had from technological efficiency, and so on.

Once one has become used to the way social scientists think about industrial organizations, one does not find this a surprising hypothesis to propose. Yet it would certainly not have been proposed in this form by any of the writers whom we discussed in the first part of this book; by Taylor, for example, who thought that everything followed from technical efficiency, or by the theorists of formal organization who stressed the importance of the work organization, or by Hawthorne investigators who emphasized morale and job satisfaction. But most of the researches which have been carried out by sociologists and social psychologists lead to a conception of the industrial organization as a system with the three major elements closely interwoven.

With these ideas in mind, the investigators studied the processes of mechanization in the coalmines of north-west Durham. The traditional method of coal-getting in this coal-field was *single-place working*. Small groups of miners worked their own place in the coal-seam. They hewed the coal from the face, loaded it into tubs, and propped up the roof as they advanced. Each miner was an all-rounder possessing the necessary skills to carry out all tasks at the face. The groups were self-selecting. They were paid according to the amount of coal they hewed *as a group*, and this was shared out equally. The fact that groups were self-selecting and each man in them could do all the jobs helped create harmonious relations in them. Relations between groups were also harmonious largely because they did not compete and because they were not subject to detailed management from above. They were capable of organizing the task of getting coal for themselves so long as management provided safe access to the workplace and the necessary services. This pattern of work organization had evolved gradually and was well adapted to the technology of single-place working.

In north-west Durham, the single-place technology was being replaced by mechanized systems of coal-getting. One of these, the *conventional longwall method*, entails strict specialization by shift. One shift undercuts a long wall of coal using a mechanical coal cutter and loosens the rest of the coal by explosive. The next shift loads the loose coal on to a moving conveyer which takes it away from the face. The task for the third shift is to prop up the roof and move the cutter and conveyer up ready for the next cutting and explosive operation. Here we see how a certain kind of work organization has been decided upon as appropriate to a certain kind of technology. The technical means available are the cutter, the explosives and the conveyer. But, as we have already seen, there is no single answer to the question: What kind of human organization is best suited to exploit these technical means in such a way as to promote social and psychological satisfaction? In this case the management had decided that specialization by shift and specialization of role were to be the chief characteristics of work organization. So that each shift, instead of comprising a number of men skilled in all the tasks required to hew and remove coal and keep the workplace safe, comprised men all of whom were skilled at one specialized task. This did not prove successful. Members of shifts were not always able to get along together when it became clear that some were more able and willing than others to perform the task. Further, specialization by shift and role called for coordination from outside the work force, to see that each shift completed its bit of the total cycle and to ensure that each member of a shift was doing his fair share of the work and cooperating with others. Whereas in single-place working the groups were self-regulating, they were now closely managed. This, as the researchers point out, is not a suitable organization for work in dangerous situations. A system of working which promotes group cohesion *is* appropriate. The outcome of this form of work organization was technical and economic inefficiency and social and psychological disturbance.

The *composite longwall method* applies a different form of work organization to the same technology. Here the multi-skilled role is introduced again and specialization minimized. The three-shift cycle obtains, but there is no sharp division of task between shifts. The team as a whole is given and accepts responsibility for the deployment of men to shifts and jobs. This is really duplicating as far as possible within longwall technology the social and psychological conditions of single-place working, i.e. group autonomy, self-regulation and multi-skilled roles. Composite working proves to be conducive to productive efficiency and social and psychological satisfaction.

The practical lesson of *Organizational Choice* is clear. If, as a manager, one has to introduce technical or administrative changes, it is wise first to work out what consequences are likely to follow from adopting one or other of the many organizational alternatives that are possible, and then to choose the one which offers the best balance of advantages. This point will be taken up and examined in more detail in Chapter 4. For the moment, we examine some of the problems attendant upon the introduction of radical changes in working practices in a British plant as these were reported by Allan Flanders.

The Fawley productivity agreement

Productivity bargaining has had a widespread application in Britain during the 1960s and 1970s. The fashion for it was largely created by managers of the Fawley Refinery of the Esso Company, and encouraged by successive British governments interested in reducing the inflationary pressure generated by collective bargaining at the workplace in conditions of full employment.

In the conditions of high unemployment of the 1980s, productivity bargaining still finds favour with employers in both private and public sectors as one means of reducing unit costs by reduced manning and the elimination of restrictive practice. This threatens the position of unions and, for that reason, they are much less enthusiastic than they were to conclude productivity agreements.

What was novel about the Fawley productivity agreements was not so much the attempt to ensure, in bargaining, that increases in pay were covered by increases in productivity, although this was unusual enough, but more that the managers at Fawley applied consciously and consistently a philosophy of industrial relations which took account of some of the things that social scientists had been saying about organizations and the people who work in them. They also took the initiative in proposing radical changes in working arrangements which cut across and threatened customary ways, in the certain knowledge that difficulties would arise; but with some confidence that they could anticipate at least some of the consequences. An account of what happened at Fawley is of particular interest for this essay. Allan Flanders was given access to the facts and his analytical description of them is set out in his book *The Fawley Productivity Agreements* (1964).

The Fawley refinery was opened in 1951. At the time of its opening it was already destined for a mention in the annals of British industrial relations. The American contractors who built the plant had insisted on negotiating with representatives of the Confederation of Unions instead of with each individual union. The success of this move in smoothing industrial relations was claimed to be a major factor in the speedy and efficient completion of the refinery, and the British Institute of Management published a short study (Gray and Abrams, 1954) which described what had happened. By the mid-fifties most of the technical bugs inevitable in a new plant had been successfully dealt with and the refinery was settling down to normal working, but at this time a number of pressures from outside persuaded the management that the efficiency of the refinery ought to be improved. The American parent company, faced with stiff price competition, had taken steps to reduce labour costs by a drastic alteration of working practices and some pruning of manpower. As a result, unfavourable comparisons were made with the situation at Fawley, where no such radical changes had been made. There were those at Fawley who were inclined to use arguments about social structure and cultural differences between Britain and the USA as an excuse for inaction. But gradually it came to be more widely felt that to allow things to remain unchanged would reflect badly upon the refinery, the British company and the professional position of the managers themselves. The need for management to take the initiative in this was argued by a small group of managers led by an energetic and knowledgeable senior executive, aided and abetted by a member of an American consulting team called in to investigate working methods. In 1958 the consultant wrote a memorandum proposing that the management should make a sharp attack upon the problem of inefficient utilization of labour. He referred chiefly to excessive overtime. Flanders describes the consultant's proposals as amounting to a high wage/low overtime policy. This was exactly the opposite of the policy which had come to be accepted in the refinery, which was that wages should be about the same as those paid for similar work in the locality but with 'superior' fringe benefits, and that overtime was necessary for technical reasons and also to satisfy the workers.

The means suggested by the consultant for achieving a high wage/low overtime situation were received with a good deal of scepticism amongst the managers because they seemed blatantly to ignore the obvious obstacles: a complicated and inflexible trade-union structure, prevailing strongly held customary interests and beliefs, and entrenched attitudes and practices. It was proposed, for example, to redeploy craftsmen's mates and to upgrade some of them to craftsmen, to amalgamate the various unskilled and semi-skilled grades into one general labouring grade, by a process of attrition to reduce the working force gradually by a third, to cut out travelling and washing time, and to introduce a forty-hour week. Impossible as most managers thought this to be, there were some who were inclined to try to work out in detail what the possible consequences of introducing such measures might be, and to begin to test out opinion amongst the men and their unions through the well-developed machinery for consultation already existing in the plant, which consisted of committees of managers, union representatives and workers at all levels who met regularly to discuss complaints, pass information, and announce proposed changes.

Up to a point the situation compares with that described by Gouldner in the work discussed earlier. Here again was a management faced with inefficient working practices buttressed by a strongly entrenched pattern of customary expectations, of a kind which Gouldner described as the indulgency pattern. But as we move away from that very general comparison to the details, the similarities disappear. At Fawley all the managers were not themselves so closely enmeshed in the customary pattern as to be incapable of cooperating in changes designed radically to disturb it, and a small group of them were eager to make changes but aware of some of the difficulties which faced them. The trade unions were much more strongly represented at Fawley, and the complicated system of collective bargaining, which in Britain goes with such representation in the multi-union plants typical of much of British industry, had no parallel in American plants. There was also the tradition in Britain that in wage negotiations it is usually the unions who take the initiative, and the existing dividing lines between manual occupations, as reflected in union demarcation lines, are inviolate. In short, the management at Fawley had bigger obstacles to overcome but were aware of the size and shape of some of them.

The Blue Book, the result of a year's work of drafting, arguing and consulting, amounted to what Flanders has described as a productivity package deal. In the process, the management detailed minutely the measures they proposed to adopt to get more efficient utilization of labour, and set out plainly what they were prepared to offer in return for the abandonment of cherished practices. They were also aware – and Flanders stresses this – of the fact that formal acceptance of the proposals by the unions did not necessarily mean that the men on the plant would find them acceptable, that they would be happy and satisfied with them. The Fawley management did not, like so many British managements, act as if once a collective agreement had been reached with union officials the job of disciplining workers into submission could be left to the unions; as if a promise by a full-time official of a trade union to put an end to a certain restrictive practice necessarily means that it will come to an end. They were aware of the need to generate at shop-floor level a conviction that changes were necessary, and a willingness to accept them in practice. Only in this way, they felt, would they create an atmosphere in which agreements reached around the bargaining table would find their full expression on the job. They also knew that even when this had been done there would still be no automatic acceptance. There would have to be lengthy explanation, protracted discussion, occasionally bitter argument, and they were not surprised when all these things happened. Yet, as Flanders points out, until forced to take notice of it, the management at Fawley overlooked 'the informal structure of organization which is intermediary between the unions and the men as individuals'. Because of this some of the consequences of the Blue Book were unanticipated and disappointing.

The arguments and difficulties which followed during the 1960s from the Blue Book and its successor, the Orange Book, as these are described by Flanders, and the social stresses and tensions generated in the process of change, once change had been accepted, demonstrate the inertial force which inheres in social institutions and in the customary expectations and practices which are its expression.

Flanders assesses the results under three headings: economic, institutional and cultural. In economic terms the aim was to raise labour productivity and distribute the gains fairly, without undue increases in cost. Institutionally, the hopes and expectations were that the productivity agreements and their consequences would demonstrate the advantages to be gained by cooperation to improve the refinery as a place of employment, as against the disadvantages of the institutionally enshrined formal haggling over trivia. Culturally, the aim was to generate a different kind of spirit in social relationships in the plant. Flanders concludes that to a considerable measure these three aims were achieved, but argues that to preserve and consolidate the situation needs continual care, attention and hard work, a better understanding of the industrial plant as a social system, and a capacity to learn this by experience.

In a chapter advancing some general conclusions of wider application Flanders draws attention to the fact so often described by social scientists that quite apart from the so-called restrictive practices of trade-union agreements, groups of workers will exercise control over their own particular working situation in what they believe to be their own best interests. Indeed, the trade-union agreements might well be the outcome of this desire to control for protective reasons. We encountered this phenomenon of group control over output and earnings in our discussion of the Hawthorne investigations. We shall, almost immediately, discuss it in more detail, in the belief that the contribution of the sociologist and social psychologist to the understanding of the behaviour of working groups is of crucial practical importance. But first we must sum up the lessons of the Fawley study.

Flanders argues, persuasively, that managers ought to take the initiative in proposing changes in working practices to improve efficiency, and in working out the implications of such changes for wages, earnings, differentials, and so on. They ought not to wait for trade unions to demand more and then find reasons for not meeting fully their demands. And the reason why this must be so is that it cannot, in reason, be shown that the unions have parity with management in managing the workplace. By reason of their technical knowledge and their power position, managers are much better placed than trade-union officials to conduct the affairs of the workplace. The role of trade unions is, *inter alia*, to criticize what managers are doing. The attitudes which are generated in the workplace by the interaction between managerial control systems and the control systems by which workers protect themselves from their possible consequences are outside the control of the unions. Yet, Flanders goes on, if this is accepted, there are social and cultural barriers to be overcome. Unless managers understand what these are, unless they have some theoretical understanding of the nature of the system they are working with, either consciously or intuitively, they are likely to fail. We are arguing here exactly the same point.

The working group and restriction of output

We referred earlier to the problem described by Taylor as systematic soldiering, i.e. group control over methods of working, levels of output and earnings, to produce output below the expectations of management. From where Taylor stood the obvious practical remedy for this was careful attention to the formal organization of division of labour and the exploitation of individual economic motives, to offset the restrictive influence of the group. As a result of the Bank Wiring Room observations and their other studies, the investigators at Hawthorne had come to a quite different set of conclusions. They said, in effect, that men at work will elaborate their relationships beyond those formally imposed by the necessities of the task in hand; in doing so, they might well develop group standards of behaviour, among which may be a norm of output lower than management expects. They will not do so consciously in pursuit of declared aims, but as a protective reaction to stimuli from the external environment of the group. If the environment is felt to be hostile a group might well control its situation in a restrictive way; if it is benign, the opposite might happen.

On this line of argument, there is no use in trying to break up groups in order to increase the output of individuals. This will merely withdraw much needed social support from the individual, affect morale, and hence performance. As a practical point, if a manager does not understand about groups and if he is faced with restriction of output, on balance he might be wise to leave well alone. If he does understand about groups, he will concern himself with the balance of advantages between leaving not-so-well alone, or taking action to create a benign group environment as far as this is within his power, while at the same time giving attention to the organizational changes which need to be made to increase output, and the effect those might have on group structure and cohesion.

From what has been said so far, it should be clear that the need to understand about groups is an essential practical asset to management. In the case of the mechanization of the coalmines of north-west Durham, much inefficiency and dissatisfaction seemed to have been caused by a failure to design working methods in tune with group values. At Fawley, the managers ran up against avoidable difficulties because they failed to take the working group sufficiently into account. Yet, in addition to those already mentioned, there have been many studies of working groups by social scientists, which for all their theoretical differences of emphasis point very much the same practical lessons. Although the findings of social science about working groups have been widely diffused, managers seem to have been slow to learn these lessons. The fault probably lies as much with the social scientists as with the managers, for not having worked hard enough to help managers apply those findings.

It seems so obvious as to be hardly worth repeating that the link between the individual and the large organization is the relationship with a small group of working colleagues, and the same might be said whether the large organization is an industrial firm, a civil service department, a hospital or a university. Yet the implications of this fact are often missed, namely that for the individual there will occur situations of conflict when there is pressure by the organization to behave in ways of which the group disapproves. When this occurs, the individual will respond mostly to the pressure of the group. However, there may arise situations in which doing what is required and valued by the group supports the formal requirements of the organization. It would therefore seem wise to attempt to find out in which circumstances this is likely to happen.

As Dubin (1962) has pointed out, the social control systems of small groups (the procedures they adopt for finding out what individuals are doing, and for bringing them into line if what they are doing offends against group norms) are much more effective than the procedures of control devised by the large organization of which the groups form a part. The organization cannot effectively police every individual item of behaviour; the group can, if it wishes. So it would seem wise, if one can create a situation in which the group perceives its environment as benign, to leave the detailed control of individual behaviour to the group; a very different conclusion from the one which Taylor advocated, but one which most of the studies reported in this section would in their various ways support. Yet the question of the steps to be taken to create a benign environment for the group still remains an open one, and the influence of technology and other facts in determining the limits of managerial action to control the environment of the group has not yet been fully explored. In the rest of this section some of the questions remaining are discussed by reference to the Bank Wiring Room and to studies carried out by the present writer (1963) and his colleagues Wilson (1962) and Cunnison (1965).

I do not intend to relate in detail the facts observed in the Bank Wiring Room at Hawthorne. These have been reported and discussed extensively elsewhere and the sources are readily available. Under observation, fourteen men engaged upon the wiring-up of terminal banks for telephone exchanges were seen to develop into a fairly cohesive group with cliques inside it, each with special interests and a special role. Certain individuals were also allocated special roles and statuses by the group. The factors determining the structure of the group and the cliques within it seemed to be the layout of the job and the formal organization of the division of labour by management (i.e. factors relating to technology) and the personal characteristics of individuals. The layout and division of labour prescribed the technologically necessary interactions between persons and these in turn led to the development of common sentiments and points of view. Some of these related to the formal organization and division of labour. Because the control of the minute details of group life by management was necessarily incomplete, there developed group controls in the interstices of the managerial control system. These controls were turned mainly to the manipulation of the incentive payment system and the level of output. The group set a ceiling on output and maintained it through its own system of booking time. So much for the facts. The observers in the Bank Wiring Room interpreted these as meaning that the processes of group formation are not willed deliberately as protective devices or as positive means to serve interests consciously perceived and formulated. Other students of these facts, and of other groups, have concluded that there are elements of deliberation in group controls in pursuit of particular interests. Roy (1954), an American student of industrial groups, remarked of one of his groups that they made noises like economic men, and this is probably the point of view implicit in Flanders's analysis of informal groups. This difference in emphasis in interpretation has its practical consequences. It is one thing to recognize a rational difference of economic interest expressed in the form of group behaviour, and another to claim that the difference of interest is a non-rational outcome of group processes. Here, I have over-stressed the contrast between two points of view in order to show

how a theoretical difference may lead to different practical policies.

The similarities between social scientists who have studied working groups are, however, of greater practical importance than the differences. Social scientists are mostly agreed about the factors which shape group structure and behaviour. These are first the technological and administrative arrangements which define necessary relations between roles (and the individual incumbents). However, as Trist *et al.* (1963) and others have pointed out, technology does not impose rigid limits on the organizational forms which might be adopted in any given case. Secondly, there are the personal characteristics of the individual incumbents of the roles. Personal characteristics here refer to the values and beliefs which the individual has learned to cherish, as well as to his mental endowment and qualities of character. If technology (broadly defined) and personal characteristics are the major determinants of group structure and behaviour, then it would follow that group structure and behaviour would tend to differ very much from organization to organization and from department to department within an organization, which is clearly so. These differences stand out sharply in my own comparative study of behaviour in two workshops, one in the electrical engineering industry and one in the garment industry.

In the electrical engineering workshop, which employed men on assembly work, the group had evolved an elaborate system of control over the level of earnings. As in the Bank Wiring Room there was much solidarity in the group as a whole, competing cliques within it, a fairly well-defined informal division of labour within the group related to the task of controlling the payment system and the allocation of work, and a system of subtle social sanctions to control the behaviour of individuals. In the garment workshop, which employed women on assembly, there was much sociability but such social cohesion as there was had not been directed to attempts to control output and earnings. The differences between the two shops may be explained by reference to a range of factors having a differential effect in the two situations, as, for example, the state of the market for the product and for labour, the technology, and the effect of these on the structuring of relationships. The system of wage payment and the methods of supervision are also relevant. So are differences in sex, the extra-factory social roles of the workers, and other individual characteristics.

These and other studies offer a guide to the things to look for when trying to explain the behaviour of groups. They are also helpful in indicating what might have to be done if group behaviour is to be changed. It is the analytical approach of the social scientist to small-group behaviour which offers most help to the practical men of affairs. Large generalizations from small studies of small groups are unhelpful.

The emphasis in this chapter has been on the analytical method of social science, and particularly sociology, rather than on particular findings of particular studies or experiments. In the final chapter an account will be given of the present state of theory about organization, and some current controversies and practical applications. It is hoped, however, that at this point the reader will be ready to follow an attempt in the next chapter to apply this analytical approach to some selected problems of industrial organization as these are customarily defined by managers. The switch is now from the world of the social scientist to the world of the manager.

4

The Manager's Problems:
What Social Science Has to Offer

The social scientist and the manager: the nature of the relationship

In earlier editions of this work I tended to regard the social scientist entirely as researcher, and his findings as being on offer to the manager. It was a matter of regret if managers were reluctant to avail themselves of what was on offer, but of no concern to the social scientist as such, although particular social scientists might prefer to devote time to practical matters. On this view, the social scientist sees himself primarily as the inhabitant of 'fields of knowledge' where the problems for research are raised by social scientists and the findings communicated amongst them in private jargon through books, articles in learned journals and conference papers. The managers' domains are 'fields of action', where practical difficulties are encountered and the means to resolve them discovered and implemented. The manager does not see it as his job to communicate his systematic reflections on his experiences in social science books and journals, although there are outstanding exceptions such as Brown (1960), Barnard (1948) and Selznick (1948). His career and reputation depend almost entirely on his success in dealing effectively and efficiently with the mostly short-term practical problems of his job. The social scientist's career *does* depend very largely on the views of other social scientists on his published output, and hardly at all on what managers think about it. Therefore, social science and the manager can only relate through the good offices of interpreters who profess to understand the 'fields of action' as well as the 'fields of knowledge'. These middlemen can tell the manager what social science has to offer, and the social scientist what the manager's problems are. This book is a good example. Here, a social scientist has taken on the role of middleman for want of someone especially trained for the role.*

My experience since I first wrote this book, as researcher, teacher and administrator in university schools of management, has convinced me that this is not the only way, or even necessarily the most effective way, to handle the relationship; although it is a valid way and will probably predominate as long as social science researchers and teachers continue to be located in organizations devoted to research and teaching, and managers in organizations devoted to making, buying, selling and distributing; one group concerned with 'fields of knowledge', the other with 'fields of action'.

This section remains an attempt to identify those difficulties that managers encounter to which the findings of social science research and reasoning might be relevant. However, it might be useful at this point to identify some other possibly fruitful ways in which social scientists and managers might relate to each other, and to give some examples.

Including the 'arm's length' mode just discussed, which may be termed the traditional mode, there are at least four kinds of possible relationship. In practice, there are many areas of overlap between them.

The traditional mode

In this mode the social scientist and the manager occupy different institutional worlds, do different things, speak different languages. Interpreters are needed to tell social scientists about managers' problems and managers about social science findings and their possible relevance.

The action research mode

In this mode, the social scientist enters the manager's world, and accepts the manager's difficulties as his own legitimate concerns. Social science knowledge is used to sharpen the focus on the problem, and on the methods of collecting and analysing relevant data. The outcome for action is a proposal to resolve the difficulty, and the outcome for social science is a set of findings, systematically arrived at, which may add to the corpus of scientific knowledge.

---

*The personnel specialist in an organization could well take on this job. This would entail some fairly radical changes in the way such specialists are trained. The case for making such changes has been argued by Lupton (1966).

An example of the latter is the idea of an open socio-technical system, to which we have already referred. This emerged out of several action researches by scientists of the Tavistock Institute in London, and is acknowledged as a major contribution to organization theory.

The organizational development mode

This can take many forms, some of which will be exemplified presently. Generally speaking, it refers to a partnership formed between managers, social scientists and others to carry out major changes in the structure and culture of a particular organization, using social science concepts and methods and developing them in the process. Some of the forms this takes may be illustrated from the experience of three companies, two British and one American.

In *Company A* organizational development started when the Board of Directors employed an eminent social scientist to be the company's organizational development adviser. Under advice, a considerable number of managers at all levels were trained as 'change agents', that is, they learned how to diffuse and to use social science concepts and methods. Armed with this body of knowledge and skills they returned to their jobs ready to help other employees discover new ways to define and solve organizational problems. Provision was made for keeping 'change agents' up to date, and for diffusing information about their experience. By this inevitably slow process a new philosophy and practice of management was developed, with beneficial effects.

Company B's Personnel Director, advised by a senior social scientist, authorized the formation of a multi-discipline team of young managers, all seconded from their regular work for two years. An experienced social science researcher joined the team as full-time adviser, and the senior social scientist acted as consultant to the team. The team was trained in social science methods and approaches, and practised them in a 'pilot' site in the company. They then offered their problem-tackling skills to managers of the company. For each project a replica of the central team would be assembled and its work directed by a member of the central team, who had been seconded to the site for that purpose. This new team would then try to solve its own problems by using methods evolved by the central team and by developing methods of its own. These teams could also spin off others of the same kind. By this process of 'cell division' it was expected that the organization would undergo permanent structural and cultural change of a radical kind over a number of years. This organization development mode is reported briefly in Lupton *et al.* (1974) and Warmington *et al.* (1977).

Company C, the American company, recruited to the Personnel Department a team of highly qualified young research psychologists and sociologists from neighbouring universities – charged first with the task of educating the personnel specialists in the methods of organization development work, and then working together with them to instruct other managers, and to help them to put the methods to practical use. The young specialists phased themselves out as and when the company's managers felt confident they could do it themselves.

Ad hoc interventions

Increasingly, social scientists have been asked, or have offered, to help managers with their problems and they have tended to approach their tasks in one or more of the following ways:

1. *Consultancy*. A social scientist might be asked, for example, to advise whether or not a company should adopt a more participative style of management or a new kind of payment system. He will probably carry out a systematic study and prepare a report with recommendations which managers will probably accept and implement. A consultant might choose to use the action research mode described above.

2. *Action learning*. Professor Revans, who was the pioneer of this method (Revans, 1980), believes that practitioners learn best from other practitioners on the job. It is helpful, therefore, if one wishes to have social science knowledge applied in practice, to second a senior manager (after a period of systematic preparation in which social scientists could be involved) to a company other than his own to investigate a particular problem, to recommend changes and, ideally, to stay around while they are introduced. There are variations in which groups (action learning sets) are allocated for problem-solving activities.

3. *Joint development activities*. Joint development activities usually take the form of a joint venture between managers in a company and university social scientists (often business school staff). The object is to combine the individual development of

the managers involved and the solution of some pressing company problem. The joint development activity (JDA) always involves some formal teaching and learning of social science ideas and methods, in addition to a project carried out in the company by the managers using social science ideas and social scientists as resources for the project. The project findings are presented to senior management. The JDA originated with Professor John Morris of the Manchester Business School. An account of a typical JDA can be found in Lupton *et al.* (1977).

Inevitably, the main mode followed in this section is the traditional mode, but wherever possible it will be shown how other modes may be used as ways of approaching the management problems treated here.

The manager's problems

Four problem-areas will be referred to:

Conflict.
Joint consultation and industrial participation.
Incentives and motivation.
Technical and administrative change.

The treatment of these will be quite brief, the assumption being that the reader will by now be sufficiently familiar with the language and general approach of social science.

Industrial conflict

For convenience of analysis, industrial conflict may be treated as being of two kinds. There are firstly those conflicts of interest, opinion and value which interfere with cooperation. Secondly, there are complete breakdowns of cooperation such as occur in strikes. In reality, as we shall argue, these are not different in kind, but different ways in which the same conflict manifests itself. We begin with the extreme case – the strike, which is a complete, but temporary, breakdown of cooperative relationships between managers and workers. If we can explain the causes of strikes, we ought to be able to indicate what might be done to avoid them or to limit them, if this is so desired. If strikes are rightly supposed to be an extreme form of non-cooperation then the explanation of go-slow, work-to-rule, restriction of output and other less violent and obvious forms of conflict will also emerge, and with it possible practical steps to be taken in dealing with them.

Gouldner, in the work previously discussed, traced one set of social processes leading to a strike. He started, as we said, by describing a small industrial unit which exhibited a stable pattern of relationships which was highly valued by all concerned. This indulgency pattern, as he called it, appeared to have emerged mainly from the influence of a benign economic environment, reinforced by the effect of kinship and neighbourliness on working relationships in the factory. The resulting customary practices and procedures were highly valued by those concerned with their operation. The indulgency pattern did not give a highly efficient use of economic and technical resources, far from it; but apparently it did give everyone a lot of satisfaction.

The attempt to abolish rapidly some of the satisfaction-giving procedures, to introduce new and more formal technical and administrative ways of doing things and of controlling the things that were done, and to appoint new men in authority to do them, generated resistance. This took the form of sabotage and of attempts to invoke formal machinery of negotiation through trade unions. The sabotage led to counter-measures which included tighter technical and administrative control, closer personal supervision of work, and the counter-use of formal machinery. The progressive break-up of the indulgency pattern was now well under way and this process became practically irreversible. More control bred more tension; adaptation took the form of counter-controls, which were countered by more formal controls, which bred more tension and more sabotage. In the absence of well-developed and subtly designed mechanisms for the redress of grievance, a complete breakdown of relationships was the inevitable result – the wildcat strike Gouldner describes. Once cooperation had broken down completely, a new process had to start to generate an atmosphere in which cooperative relations could be resumed and social mechanisms established for the redress of future grievances.

If one were to hazard a generalization at this stage it would be that attempts at radical administrative or technical change, without regard to the provision of social mechanisms for dealing with their consequences, bid fair to end in social breakdown. What these social mechanisms are and how they may be introduced is left for later discussion. However, some things stand out clearly from Gouldner's analysis of the gypsum factory case and from many other studies. One of these is that the attempt to design a new management structure and new working practices, and to introduce them as if they only had to be explained to be acceptable, is likely to fail. Paradoxically, although such attempts might seem rational means to economic ends supposedly desired by everybody, they might well set in motion social processes leading to a complete breakdown of cooperation.

In the case described by Gouldner it was the introduction of formal administrative procedures of control which started the process. But we saw, when we considered the work of Joan Woodward and of the Liverpool University team, that the nature of the production technology might have an effect on role expectations and on the way in which technological change is assimilated. So we must not say that strikes or other forms of non-cooperation will necessarily follow technical and administrative change. If, for example, the technology is such as to afford some intrinsic satisfaction in the job, if there are well-developed formal methods for joint negotiation and for handling disputes, if there is time to use the machinery, and if the general social and economic environment is such as to encourage goodwill, then people may well cooperate in the process of change. In the steelworks studied by the Liverpool team, the situation had many of these features.

Economic logic and the nature of conflict

Usually, the rational economic logic begins with an assessment of current and likely future demands for products and services. Decisions then follow stating what will be provided in what quantities and at what price to satisfy those demands. After this the technical and administrative means to that end must be explored, as well as questions about how the responsibility for performing the necessary tasks should be formally allocated, how work flow is to be planned, scheduled and controlled, and how expenditures are to be recorded and controlled. For brevity's sake we will refer to these and other such means as *production arrangements*. From the production arrangements may be logically derived *job requirements*, i.e. those individual skills, patterns of activity and consequent relationships between jobs and their occupants that are needed to make the production arrangements work as planned. The outcome of the rational economic logic may be referred to as a *structure* of roles and role relationships.

It is possible, of course, that the structures so derived will turn out to be entirely consistent with the outcomes of another set of processes of reasoning, evaluation and choice, which have given rise to ideas of what the structure and the individual job requirements *should be* if they are to satisfy what the occupants or potential occupants of the jobs consider their legitimate aspirations and expectations to be. These would typically refer to absolute and relative level of income, the quality of interpersonal relationships, progress in careers, the personal satisfaction to be gained from work, and the way in which authority is exercised. They often turn out to be a good deal more complex and subtle than that, and, consequently, not easily accessible to the inquirer. As we saw in Gouldner's study, the outcomes of economic reasoning do not always turn out to be consistent with the outcomes of the second process which has its origins in the family role, in educational and work experience, in the current state of the labour market, in the policies of trade unions, all matters outside the immediate influence of the economic reasoners. Many of the problems of management arise from the inconsistency of the two sets of outcomes. It is plain that if there is considerable inconsistency then there will be reluctance by individuals and groups to activate the planned production arrangements. This will in turn frustrate the planned response to the market in the products or services.

What can managers do in such circumstances? There are three possible ways of coping. *Firstly*, during the sequence of decisions which make up the economic logic, opportunities should be taken to choose alternative product ranges and production arrangements, for example, in such a way that the resulting job requirements are as consistent as possible with what is known of actual and potential job expectations and aspirations. This demands that the latter can be known and that there is a desire to know them. Managers trained only in the specialized aspects of the economic logic – as, for example, assessors and forecasters of markets, designers of production systems, accountants, production planners, or work study engineers – are unlikely to have developed systematic methods of gaining access to such knowledge and taking account of it. *Secondly*, on the assumption that the outcomes of economic logic are by definition best for everyone concerned because they are designed to increase the sum total of economic wealth available for sharing, which is assumed to be the sole *raison d'être* of organization, then anything which is, or appears to be, inconsistent is either due to innocent ignorance or forgivable irrationality, or both. In that case, processes of beneficial training and education to eradicate ignorance and to diffuse economic rationality seem to be indicated. This, in essence, is the position of the scientific management movement. *Thirdly*, and more commonly perhaps, the experiences of managers, especially those who are general managers and not the specialists referred to above, lead them to accept the high probability of inconsistency, and to create structures and processes which enable aspirations and expectations to be articulated openly and endorsed as legitimate. The problem to be faced is now defined and can perhaps be tackled by negotiation or by dialogue exploring the possibilities for consensus about values, through a search for alternatives within the economic logic and acceptable ways to influence the processes by which expectations and aspirations are formed.

The social scientist's recommendation for the management of structural conflict would probably be a mixture of the first and third of the tactics which have just been referred to. When changes are being made (and most industrial and commercial organizations are continually undergoing change), the manager must find a way of influencing the interconnections within and between the two logics so as to achieve that balance of economic, social and psychological values, which is most consistent with the continued growth and development of the organization and the individuals employed in it. Both the findings and methods of investigation of social science are useful tools in that endeavour, as we shall see in Chapter 5.

Before going on to discuss another type of conflict-generating situation, it is necessary to deal with a possible objection to the argument so far. What about human malice, stupidity, irrationality? What about agitators, and people who are so daft that they cannot see where their own best interests lie? Is not this kind of thing the cause of most of the troubles of management? Do we need all this stuff about role expectations and social structure? Take agitators first. Social scientists are not the only people who think systematically about social situations. If a person has an intuitive grasp of the fact that processes which threaten eventual social breakdown have been induced, and he is convinced that this is a good thing because it will embarrass his enemies, then if he is able to do so he will take steps, more or less skilfully, to hasten the process. Naturally, he will come up against those who do not want the process to go on, and name-calling ensues. The name-calling is an effect, not a cause. As for daft people who cannot see where their own best interests lie, it would seem that persons and groups come to define their own best interests from their shared social experience. They do not on the whole take kindly to statements from others that if they took this or that factor into account, they would soon see that they were mistaken. They might, however, change if their social experience changed.

Straight conflicts of economic interest, which we distinguish from structural conflicts, are the result of a deliberate decision to coerce employers in one way or another to part with more cash or power, or to give better working conditions. It is not being suggested here that strikes are *either* the result of tensions arising from frustrated role expectations *or* of decisions to try open coercion when other means have failed. Both elements are likely to be present in any strike. What *is* being suggested is that where there are conflicts about pay, there are also procedures for bargaining about pay and for avoiding a breakdown of cooperation emerging from failure to agree, and there are fairly rational means for dealing with conflicts of interest. Sometimes, the machinery proves incapable of handling the demands made upon it, and open coercion is employed. As every student of collective bargaining knows, the hidden sanction of strike or lockout always underlies bargaining. But usually industrial conflict is both a structural conflict and an interest conflict; indeed, it is only possible to separate the two analytically, never in practice.

When we discussed Flanders's study of changes in working practices at Fawley we saw how problems arose from the formal clash of interests over pay and conditions with trade union officials, and how the managers tried to anticipate, with some success, the social structural effects of change on the attitudes of the workers themselves. If the managers had not done so, if they had seen the only problem of administrative change as the negotiation of new wage rates, new job definitions and so on through the formal machinery, they might possibly have set in train the circular process of structural tension, sabotage, tight control, tension, sabotage, etc. But they tried not only to anticipate the structural effects of the changes they were proposing. They also tried to prepare people for these changes. The same kind of procedure was adopted by the managers in the Liverpool steelworks study. What is being done here, in effect, is to create a special temporary structure of role relationships for preparing for, and handling the consequences of, structural change. It was the absense of awareness of the need for this machinery of social transition, and of opportunities to create it, which was part of the difficulty in the gypsum factory.

The practical lessons of all this are quite clear. Firstly, managers ought not to rely too heavily on formal machinery for settling conflicts of economic interest in conditions of social and administrative change. At least, they ought to examine this machinery to see if it seems adequate to handle the structural consequences of change. They ought also to consider seriously what additional social mechanisms can be created to ease the transition. Later, in a discussion of joint consultation, we will be discussing this point more fully.

A third kind of conflict which we have to discuss is that arising from dissatisfaction with the job itself. It has been argued persuasively from empirical evidence that good environmental conditions – so-called job hygiene, i.e. good welfare facilities, meals, lighting, heating, good mates – are not as important in promoting satisfaction in work as the actual job itself. Yet, it is often economically and technologically necessary, as in the situation described by Walker and Guest, so to divide the total task in pursuit of productive efficiency that each individual job offers little or no satisfaction. If we assume that people expect their jobs to give them satisfaction, then we should also expect that to do unsatisfying work day in and day out might lead to protest. The protest could take the form of an individual decision to leave and get another job. It could take the form of attempts, either by individuals or groups, to provide in the job situation some compensating satisfactions, such as pitting wits against management on piecework rates. Or it could take the form of periodic stoppages of work. It is difficult to say, because this would depend upon circumstances, just what form the protest might take, but (again assuming that people expect to get satisfaction from their jobs) a manager might well anticipate some kind of protest in reaction. This element of job dissatisfaction might enter also into structural conflict. The tension generated by frustrated social expectations might be heightened by 'fed-upness' with the job itself. All this suggests that it would be unwise for a manager to rely too much on the effects of welfare facilities, or even high wages, to offset the frustrating effects of unsatisfying jobs. To allow scope for workers to develop their own compensating mechanisms might be much better. It is possible that, as Goldthorpe *et al.* have argued (1968), some industrial workers do not expect their jobs to be satisfying, but regard the hours spent at work as unpleasant interludes yielding income which enables them to seek satisfaction elsewhere.

There is some evidence – which would tell against this line of argument – that restrictive practices, which are a form of restricted cooperation, arise from attempts by workers to do two things: first, to protect their long-term sectional economic interests and, second, to compensate for the unsatisfactory nature of the work, or the uncertainties in management planning, by individual or group control over the work. The practical solution to this problem is difficult. To attempt root and branch administrative reform might promote structural conflict, conflict of economic interest, and dissatisfaction with the job and the relationships involved in it. The task of the manager is to think out a line of action which offers scope for job satisfaction, and/or scope for compensating control, and which at the same time leads to technical and administrative efficiency. This sounds very difficult, and rather than attempt it many managers would argue that it is sufficient to provide a forum where men can air their grievances and management can inform them of what it proposes to do, and to try in general to promote a sense of loyalty to the company and a feeling of mutual interest. Some of the practical shortcomings of the sense of belonging and mutual-interest approach will have become apparent by now. In the next short section we discuss them in more detail.

To sum up, organizational conflict is the likely outcome of attempts to organize cooperation in situations of technical and economic complexity. It can manifest itself as structural conflict; conflict for scarce resources of cash and the power to influence events; or conflict arising from protest against boring, monotonous work. Actual conflict may well emerge as a mixture of the three, when an organization is confronted with the need to change its technology or its administrative procedures. Some industries seem more prone to conflict of all three kinds than others. There is evidence that mining and dock work, wherever in the world one finds them, are conflict-prone. Other industries, such as textiles, seem less so. This is probably because the environment in which strife-ridden industries are living is less benign. The economics of dock work, prey to tides, weather and the vagaries of world shipping, combined with geographic isolation which promotes cohesion amongst a casual labour force, go far to explaining the high incidence of conflict. They do not go all the way. Examples of a low incidence of conflict in an industry normally conflict-prone can be found, the outcome of successful attempts to overcome the disadvantages of the environment. It is also possible for managers and workers to develop ill-will when all the external circumstances are favourable to goodwill and cooperation. Yet the opportunities obviously differ greatly, and it is clear that some managers who want to limit, guide and control the level of conflict will encounter more difficulties than others. The social scientist is able to point out the likely result of certain external conditions, such as location, technology, labour markets and product markets, in creating the conditions for conflict. With this knowledge the manager may take the measure of his problems and begin to estimate the likely success of this or that change in policy.

The management of conflict

Managers, and other employees of organizations, recognize that conflicts of the kind we have been discussing are likely to occur at some level of frequency and intensity. Because managers are responsible for the efficient use of the resources in their charge, they are particularly anxious to minimize the economic impact of conflict. They have therefore sought ways to reduce the incidence of conflict and to minimize its economic, social and psychological effects when it does arise. Non-managerial employees, who also experience negative effects of conflict, have sought formal (sometimes legal) means to ensure their greater involvement in decisions that affect their economic interests and their working conditions, and access to information relevant to those interests. In this section we explore some of the recommended ways of seeking to avoid, anticipate and cope with conflict. They range from the re-structuring of management systems and the modification of individual managerial behaviour via training and development, through formal committees and procedures to the design of socio-technical systems and individual jobs. We start with the simpler and best-known.

Joint consultation and participation

The term 'joint consultation' is usually used to describe the formal machinery through which the managers and the workers in a firm, or their elected or appointed representatives, discuss their common problems, decide about them and exchange information. In some firms there is no such formal machinery. Where it does exist, it differs much from firm to firm. And in the majority of cases a sharp distinction is drawn between the machinery of joint consultation and the machinery of collective bargaining. This section is not intended to be a detailed description of the practice of joint consultation and it will examine the question of worker participation in decision making and management in a much wider context. It might be useful, however, before looking at joint consultation and participation in the light of social science findings, to describe a typical example.

In a small firm, joint consultation might take place in a works committee, composed of elected or appointed workers representing departments, and managers nominated by the chief executive or serving in rotation. The worker representatives may or may not be union shop stewards, depending on whether the union is strong, and on its views about joint consultation. In a large firm there may be departmental committees dealing with local matters and sending agenda items and representatives forward to a larger committee at works level. The agenda of all committees will usually exclude topics considered to be matters for the collective bargaining machinery. The items remaining could well include the consideration of productivity figures and proposals for improvement, welfare services and canteens, the administration of a profit-sharing scheme, or exchanging information about the firm's market position and economic problems. Rarely would they lead to decisions encroaching on managerial prerogatives.

In its most common expression, the theory of joint consultation comprises a few straightforward propositions about human nature and industrial organization. It is held, firstly, that individuals feel better if they are given an opportunity, either directly or indirectly, at the most to participate in those decisions which affect their jobs and hence their living, at the least to be informed of what decisions have been taken and why. The second hypothesis is that an organization wishing to keep its employees satisfied should provide a forum where they can voice their minor grievances and canvass ideas for improvements. Thirdly, while it might be admitted that there are issues and occasions for conflict in industry, there are also many more points of common interest and objective between managers and workers than are normally explicit in the day-to-day business of getting the job done, and joint consultation helps to provide the means to seek common ground. Fourthly, there are many matters of administration, of sports clubs, bonus and profit-sharing schemes and the like, where the organizing talents of the ordinary employee can find opportunities denied to him unavoidably in everyday work. Fifthly, it is usually supposed that if the facilities for participation and the forum for discussion are provided, the employees will feel better about working for the firm. The result then will be lower turnover and absence rates, a lower incidence of conflict, a feeling of loyalty and belonging, and in all probability a greater will to work. Finally, joint consultation allows managers and workers to meet in circumstances where their relationship of subordinate to superior is played down, and their common role as employees of the firm, equally concerned with its fortunes, is played up, and this, it is claimed, is good for everyone's morale.

One can cite examples where a formal system of committees, designed to give effect to these theories and taken seriously by the management of the firm, has worked in the sense that it has engaged the interest of the employees at least to the point where they are prepared to vote, to stand for elections, and in general to become in some way involved. But it is difficult to measure exactly the effect of such a system. It is easy therefore for the sceptic to point to the impossibility of isolating the effect of joint consultation from all the other effects on relationships within the firm, or to argue that perhaps the apparent success of joint consultation is the effect and not the cause of harmonious relationships. It is possible to cite even more examples where joint-consultation systems were set up only to fall speedily into disuse for lack of interest or of things to discuss, and even more where the committees carry on as management tribunals for the periodic hearing of the minor grievances of the shop floor and the announcement of management intentions. To refer back to the theory does not help explain the successes, the failures or the scepticism. Is there anything in social science which does?

In answer to that question we may refer to what social scientists have to say about the causes and consequences of employee participation, to inquire whether there is anything there which would support the common-sense theory previously summarized, and if there is what it implies for practical policy. We may also ask whether social scientists have any way in which they can measure the effect of adopting or not adopting this or that system of joint consultation or employee participation. However, before we do this we might as well say that the simple practical reason why joint consultation is often introduced is a belief that the industrial firm should practise some form of democracy. Since no great harm is likely to ensue from the attempt to do so, it is easy to indulge in it, and it is unimportant whether it exists alongside high labour turnover, unofficial strikes and the like, which occur, it is believed, for reasons other than the presence or absence of democracy.

Probably the most serious practical attempt to explore the relationship between industrial efficiency and industrial democracy and to devise means to combine them took place at the Glacier Metal Company in London. It would use much more space than I have at my disposal to describe this exploration in detail, but the main outlines of the theory and practice are clear. At Glacier they subscribed up to a point to the theories of formal organization which we discussed earlier. They argued the value of clarity of role definition and role relationships, and the importance of avoiding confusion arising from conflicting definitions of the same activity (for example, what management is), and aimed to clear away misunderstanding about words and symbols. They sought to devise efficient formal systems of authority, responsibility and function, and patterns of communication, and looked for equitable ways of deciding differential rewards for work done. All this was done carefully and systematically, using concepts derived from the social sciences. In pursuit of efficiency they tried to build a stable structure of formal role expectations, which embodied a written code of rules governing behaviour and relationships. The social analysts at Glacier Metal were interested in the question which Gouldner raised, namely, who makes the rules in bureaucracies and what effect this knowledge has on the attitudes of employees.

After a good deal of detailed action research* on the working of orthodox joint consultation in situations where rule-making was almost entirely a management prerogative, it came to be believed that relationships in the firm would become much more harmonious and effective if the making of rules governing behaviour was jointly undertaken by committees representing all grades and skills – a legislative system – and if once the rules were made the management were entirely responsible to the legislators for administering them effectively – the executive system. The attempt was made to extend this system of democratic management throughout the company, in such a way that the autonomy of small units within

* Research which is directed towards the practical improvement of the situation under observation.

the company to decide and act was pushed as far as was consistent with overall coordination and the use of specialist services. The merits claimed for this system are that it allows free play to the desire of men to participate, however humbly, in matters affecting their work; it provides channels through which people can learn quickly the consequences of decisions and take appropriate action; it affirms managerial authority; and it creates an atmosphere where people feel free to express themselves knowing that redress against arbitrary authority is to be had. In all, it removes some of the inequalities and injustices which generate tension, uneasiness and distrust, making it possible for people to work effectively in roles which are clearly defined and equitably rewarded.

Here, at Glacier Metal, is an example of a collaboration of a rather unusual kind between social scientists and managers over many years. Workers and managers were involved in a continuous process of analysis of the organization and many changes came about as a result. The outcome of this collaboration (Jaques, 1951; Jaques, 1956; Brown, 1960) deserves the attention of all practising managers and social scientists. There is, however, a danger that the uncritical propagation of the Glacier system as a general set of principles of management might lead to exact imitation in situations where it is inappropriate, or where the personal skills required by managers are lacking. There is also a danger that the underlying value premise of the Glacier work will be uncritically accepted, namely that it is part of the responsibility of industrial managers to promote industrial harmony, to play down conflict and tensions, on the ground that to do so leads to industrial efficiency and that it promotes emotional security and a sense of belonging, and that both of these are good. Another equally valid but contrasting premise might be that the task of management is to allow considerable free play to individual and sectional interests and to set up machinery for avoiding the worst consequences of the rational pursuit of sectional self-interest. The basic assumption in this case would be that managers ought to manage according to rules which serve their interests, and workers ought to have scope to resist those consequences of management which affect their interests.

The Glacier Metal project is in the Hawthorne tradition in taking the view that the task of management is not just a technical one. Management is also a job of creating a social organization in which everyone may participate to the greatest possible degree and with which everyone may feel a sense of close identification. In the same tradition stand Likert (1967) and his associates, McGregor (1960), Argyris (1957), Blake and Mouton (1961), and Herzberg, Mausner and Snyderman (1959). These names, and the ideas and prescriptions for action that are associated with them, are becoming more widely known and accepted amongst British managers. They therefore merit discussion here.

Let us accept that each human being has inborn capacities for development. Whether he does or does not develop to the limit of his capacities, and in what directions, will depend on the social environment in which he grows up. Let us also accept that if human beings are to be effective and happy they have certain needs that must be satisfied – needs for food, clothing and shelter certainly, but also for acceptance and recognition by their fellows and for individual self-expression, and not least a need to have some control over matters that affect their welfare as they themselves interpret it. A number of things follow: firstly, if we are to release all the talents that individuals are capable of then we must create environments for them that allow these talents expression. Secondly, if individuals are to work together effectively and happily then we must create environments which satisfy individual needs for self-expression, acceptance and social recognition. Thirdly, that if environments are *not* created that satisfy human needs individuals will either sink into unproductive apathy, try themselves to create their own supportive environment, or revolt openly against that environment.

The modern industrial organization is an environment in which many human beings spend a large proportion of their waking hours. Managers are largely the creators of that environment. Therefore it is not only incumbent upon managers, as a social duty, to provide an environment in which individual needs may be met and individual talents flower; it also makes good economic sense. Individuals will not behave protectively and restrictively in such an environment and therefore will readily cooperate, and make available all the usable skills and competences that the organization can recognize and develop.

Is the argument just outlined merely a belief or is there good evidence to support the theoretical propositions embedded in it? To answer this question is of practical significance. If the evidence is convincing then we can proceed to the practical questions of how the supportive stimulating environments may be created.

McGregor, in his book *The Human Side of Enterprise* (1960), draws a sharp distinction between two views of human nature and organization. The first view, which McGregor refers to as Theory X, claims that efficiency follows from the pursuit of clear objectives set by high authority, carried through by tight impersonal managerial control over individual performance, and buttressed by punitive sanctions, usually economic. The practical expression of this kind of theory is found in scientific management and the principles of formal organization. However, McGregor says that it is by no means evident that individuals will only work effectively if they are subjected to tight control or the lure of cash. We may have been deluded into thinking so by interpreting the observed attempts of individuals and groups to escape through the mesh of tight management control, as conclusive evidence of the need for tighter control. The opposite equally plausible view, which McGregor calls Theory Y, is that if individuals are invited to take part in setting the standards they are to work towards, if they are given tasks which catch their enthusiasm and engage their talents, and if they feel, and are in fact, free to help create and develop the environment in which they work, and that the rewards to them for doing so are justly distributed, then they will work effectively and happily together.

McGregor's is a popular not a scientific book, and it does not therefore systematically assemble the evidence in support of Theory Y nor does it assemble and criticize systematically the evidence for Theory X. However, there *is* evidence from the Hawthorne experiments which suggests a bias in favour of Theory Y, and Theory Y certainly harmonizes better with those aspects of Western political ideology which stress freedom of choice, participation, equality and innovation, as against those that emphasize order, control and continuity. This is why many managers who have read McGregor, or who have heard his ideas discussed, tend to describe themselves as Theory Y men, or at least to think that they ought to try harder to be Theory Y men.

Blake and Likert, in common with McGregor, see the answer to the problem of creating the organization environment for maximum performance and human satisfaction at work as lying largely in the style or pattern of management, i.e. they take the view that the sets of attitudes and the personal behaviour of managers are the mainsprings of effective organizational performance. That is to say that if one wants deliberately to influence organizational performance, then it would be managerial style that one would wish to change, or more correctly, it would be management style that one would start with, in the confident expectation that other beneficial changes would follow.

Blake and Mouton in their book *The Managerial Grid* and Likert in *The Human Organization* approach the task of identifying and defining managerial styles in similar ways. Blake starts with a classification of managerial styles. There are, he avers, two variables: concern for people and concern for production. Nine points on two orthogonal scales, each of which represents one variable, produce a grid giving eighty-one combinations of concern for people and concern for production. Blake selects five of these combinations, those scoring 1/1, 1/9, 9/1, 9/9 and 5/5 for consideration. He asks us to accept that 9/9 is the preferred managerial style, preferred in the sense that it leads to good economic and socio-psychological results. It is possible, using a questioning technique devised by Blake, for managers in a company to identify the position of themselves or their organization on the grid. If it is not 9/9 then it is clear the improvements must come from a move in the direction of 9/9. Blake prescribes how the movement may be effected, e.g. by T Group-like* experiences cutting across the formal lines of authority, and then by joint identification of the tasks to be performed and by the structuring relationships appropriate to the tasks that are psychologically satisfying and economically effective.

Blake's managerial grid procedure has been on the whole accepted as useful by managers. His method of classification has so far escaped serious criticism (although Reddin has added a third dimension of effectiveness), and I personally have heard few managers question the factual evidence adduced by Blake in support of the proposition that 9/9 management style is conducive to economic performance and job satisfaction.

The logical foundations of Blake's method and the evidence he gives in support of his position as to the relationship between managerial style and organizational performance are unconvincing to me. However, if I were a manager I might be attracted by Blake's procedure as a systematic way of opening up discussion in the organization on the connection between managerial behaviour

---

* T Group means, literally, a training group. It usually takes the form of placing people in an unstructured setting, i.e. with no set rules or authority structure and no task other than to try to understand how groups work so that they may directly experience, observe and subsequently analyse the processes by which men come into conflict and cooperate, and examine, critically, in a supportive atmosphere, their own beliefs, attitude and prejudices.

and organizational success. The procedure is also straightforward, uncluttered and practical, and its value premises – that it is good for a manager to be concerned about people and about production, and that it is possible to be concerned about both at the same time without contradiction or conflict – are most attractive.

Likert's work is based on extensive and intensive professional research over many years. He and his research team at Michigan carried out many studies with the object of establishing the nature of the relationship between management and supervisory style, on the one hand, and the performance and satisfaction of cooperating individuals on the other. From this work Likert has distilled four recognizable systems of management, i.e. he has evolved, like Blake, a classification of management styles (or more accurately in Likert's case, patterns of managerial attitudes, beliefs and behaviour). These are presented as profiles showing a characteristically different set of scores on forty-three items defining management systems from 1 to 4 as follows:

System 1. Exploitive – authoritative
System 2. Benevolent – authoritative
System 3. Consultative
System 4. Participative – group

System 4, as its brief description indicates, includes a style of management that favours employee involvement in managerial decisions and an open system of communications designed to engender trust and confidence. It also regards the working group as a potentially powerful positive force for efficiency and a source of employee satisfaction, and as such a significant 'building block' of organization. System 4 has some similarities with 9/9 management, but it explicitly includes more organizational factors.

Likert's research findings show a marked tendency for System 4 to be associated with high economic efficiency and also high job satisfaction. However, he also reports examples where such associations are found with the other three systems, and where System 4 shows no such associations. The research did not take account of other factors such as technology and rate of structural change, which might have explained the apparent lack of uniformity in the findings. Likert therefore feels justified in setting them aside and in arguing that on the balance of evidence, a move from any other system to System 4 would be generally beneficial. He also prescribes how such moves are best made.

Whatever the detailed differences between McGregor, Blake and Likert, I believe their approach to management to be almost exactly similar. They consider the individual worker or manager as the unit for investigation, and their starting point is that they all have certain needs to be satisfied and talents to be utilized. Whether the needs will be satisfied or the talents released will depend on the environment that is created for the individual. Since managers are the creators of the environment of other managers and workers, then the attitudes, beliefs and behaviour of managers are of overwhelming significance for organizational performance. These writers then go on to classify styles and systems of management – 81 styles for Blake, 2 theories for McGregor, and 4 Systems for Likert. They all array evidence to show which style, theory or system is superior as a vehicle for improvement. Finally, they show how, having identified that a particular company's management does not come out as 9/9, Theory Y or System 4, a movement in that direction may be started. In each case the method is primarily one of inculcating, by various training procedures, a new set of attitudes and resulting patterns of behaviour. This general approach might be described as psychological universalism, since it rests on the notion that the principles and procedures evolved apply to all individual–organization relationships, regardless of the characteristics of particular organizations.

Argyris might also be described as a psychological universalist, yet his emphasis is less, it would seem, on the *styles of management* appropriate to high organizational performance and satisfaction (although he is certainly interested in that), than on the *forms of organization structure* that seem likely to be appropriate in meeting individual needs and promoting interest, enthusiasm and creativity. Argyris in many books and articles has argued that hierarchical organizations using rigid work-flow controls and financial motivation will stunt and deprive the individual, or lead to individual or collective protective–restrictive practices (both amongst managers and workers) which reduce organizational performance. For this reason Argyris prefers organizations that are flexible and project-based, and where relationships in management are collegiate rather than hierarchical.

This brief, and necessarily inadequate, review of the practical implications of the school of psychological universalists cannot be concluded without reference to Frederick Herzberg, since his ideas have certainly been attractive to many British managers who have come into contact with them. Herzberg's concern, in his researches, was to establish the causes of job satisfaction and dissatisfaction. The interviews on which he originally based his conclusions, reported in *The Motivation to Work*, were mainly with professional men, engineers and accountants. These studies have since been replicated with similar groups and different groups both by Herzberg *et al.* (1959) and by others. Some of the results confirm Herzberg's view, some do not. However, Herzberg's own initial caution about the practical conclusions that could justifiably be drawn from his work have passed unnoticed in the enthusiasm to take up his ideas.

The ideas themselves, based on the original findings, are attractive to common sense. People want the satisfaction of being recognized, doing a job that carries responsibility, a chance to get into more interesting and challenging work, opportunities to be stretched, and so on; in short the satisfactions for the individual are intrinsic to the job itself. To be sure, people grumble about the pay, the working conditions, and the people they work with and for, but these are not the factors which positively move them to higher performance. We have, therefore, a set of dissatisfiers – things which will cause grumbling if they are not up to standard but which will not positively motivate – and a set of satisfiers, that are intrinsic to the job and which increase motivation. We have come across this general idea before. Its practical consequence is not, of course, that pay, pension rights and one's colleagues are unimportant and can be neglected; it is that if the object is to allow people to grow to the size of which they are capable one has to give them room. This means devising jobs that offer people a challenge, not just enlarging a job so that a person has more similar things to do, but enriching it so that it offers him more positive opportunities to fulfil himself as an individual in his work.

The work of the psychological universalists adjures the manager to create an environment in which individuals can fulfil themselves in jobs rich with challenge, and can participate in decisions that are going to affect them. This prescription, they argue, is not woolly human relations but good practical economic sense; for is it not obvious that if the people who make up an organization are interested in what they are doing, are enthusiastic about it, and are using all their skills and competences fully, and given that the structure and style of management is appropriate, then that organization will be a successful organization?

This view, however attractive it may appear, is open to criticism. It is not untrue in the sense that it lacks conclusive supporting evidence – most theories and prescriptions about organization and management could be criticized for that – but it is over simple and incomplete and, for that reason, misleading for managers who expect the social sciences to offer guides to improved practice. There is scant reference to factors which are known to give rise to difficulties for managers, factors concerned with organizational size and structural complexity, for example. Nor are the consequences of the nature of technology given much weight. The manager who is in charge of a capital-intensive process plant is likely to face different problems from one running a complex, labour-intensive, manufacturing assembly operation, not to mention the difference in costs and the logistics associated with changing a given technology to one where greater concern for people is to be a weightier consideration than hitherto. When labour is plentiful and willing to work in existing conditions, and where trade unions have more urgent priorities than job satisfaction and employee participation in the workplace, there is no pressure on employers to change, especially in conditions where market demand is sluggish and cash for development difficult to come by. In such conditions the argument that restructuring jobs, or altering management styles, is the main key to productive efficiency is not likely to gain many sympathetic hearers amongst employers and senior managers, even if it were generally true that it is applicable in all organizational settings. Perhaps even more seriously, the doctrines could well be bound by culture, i.e. the prescriptions are based on the aspirations and beliefs of modern North Americans. To apply them to less developed, less affluent societies could have the effect of making people less satisfied with their jobs and less productive. Whether that would or would not be the effect has yet to be demonstrated.

The circumstances which will tempt employers to embrace the doctrines which associate 9/9 management style, job enrichment, System 4 and suchlike things with satisfaction at work and productive efficiency would seem to be some combination of the following factors:

Tight labour markets.
Buoyant product markets.
Product-market uncertainties.
A highly educated work force in the labour market

High rate of economic growth.
Availability of investment capital.

If organizations have difficulty in attracting educated people into the factory or office because jobs there are reputed to be boring and monotonous and the management style authoritarian, and if at the same time the product is in high demand at current prices and investment capital is available at reasonable rates of interest, it might make economic sense to restructure the work to make it attractive and to remodel management structures and styles accordingly. There is, however, a risk that such moves might increase costs and reduce competitiveness in the product market.

In some European countries during the 1960s and 1970s a small number of large manufacturing companies moved in this direction. Sweden, Holland and West Germany are notable amongst them, but examples can be found in France, Italy, Norway, Denmark and, to a lesser extent, the United Kingdom. Assembly lines were dismantled and replaced by production systems which featured extended time-cycles for jobs, greater control of the job by the worker, and the establishment of the work group as a unit of work-flow management. Research by Lupton and Tanner (1980a) which attempted to trace the causes and consequences of these developments revealed that the designers were little influenced by the doctrines of Likert, Blake and Herzberg, or indeed social scientists of any kind. Such writers were not a significant influence on the managers and engineers who conceived and built the many brilliant alternatives to the conventional assembly line now to be found in manufacturing companies in Europe, such as Philips, Volvo, Bosch, Olivetti and Renault. It is possible, however, that the Scandinavians were more consciously influenced than the others by the doctrines we have referred to and by the Tavistock Institute researches.

The search for new kinds of manufacturing systems was, it seems, triggered by simultaneous pressures from the product market and the labour market. The nature of the demand had created a need for more flexibility of response than the assembly line was able to give, and indigenous labour was in short supply. Unions were also asking for better jobs, and society generally for a better quality of working life. Designers found themselves searching for reliable designs which would give a flexible response to market changes at low unit cost and with high quality, and simultaneously provide workers with satisfying jobs in pleasant surroundings. The economic aims on the one hand, and the social and psychological aims on the other, were not always easy to reconcile and methods had to be found to effect this reconciliation. Some of these are discussed in detail in Chapter 5 (Lupton, 1975; Aguren and Edgren, 1980).

More recently, changes in product markets, labour markets and capital markets, together with the acceleration in the development of labour-saving technologies, have shifted the emphasis away from job design and modifications of the structure of technology and work organization. Now organizational decentralization and worker participation seem to be more acceptable means to improve motivation and increase economic efficiency. In general, then, it is unwise to advance proposals for the improvement of the quality of working life which do not specify the conditions under which they are likely to succeed in their aims, and how these aims can be reconciled with economic, organizational and societal exigencies in practical ways. Otherwise managers will either ignore them, adopt them uncritically and run the risk of failure and disillusionment, or turn to different prescriptions for efficiency and satisfaction only to find that they too are theoretically over simple and present, in consequence, problems in application.

Economic incentive and motivation

The ideas of joint consultation, job design and participative management which we have just been discussing may also be seen as ideas about incentive and motivation. They explain how to structure situations so that the people in them will be moved to behave cooperatively. Metaphorically, they show how to breathe life into formal structures designed to achieve particular objectives. But there are other kinds of incentive, which are much better known and much more frequently resorted to by managers as a means to higher outputs by workers. I refer, of course, to cash incentives.

When we examined the work of Taylor, we argued that scientific management rests on a belief that managers and workers have an underlying mutual interest in cooperating effectively with each other. It is only because of lack of forethought by managers that this mutual interest is obscured. According to the tenets of scientific management, the recognition of mutual interest is achieved by a division of labour between managers and operatives in which managers do the planning and organizing and operators do the operating. The responsibility of management, so the argument goes, is to manage, which means to make the best possible use of the resources at its disposal to achieve the objectives set. Operators have an interest in efficient management because it can create more wealth to share out than inefficient management. This interest can never be a direct one because it is inefficient to have operators, who are not trained to plan, to organize and to coordinate, interfering with these proper concerns of management. Therefore it is part of the task of management, which it has an obligation to perform efficiently, to define for the operator exactly what is expected of him, and to provide him with the equipment and services necessary to meet these expectations. If the operator is properly selected and trained for the task, then the result of the division of labour between the organizers and the doers ought to result in high outputs, and this makes it possible to give high rewards for the performance of the task. It is this relation, between a clearly defined task and a clearly defined and (notionally) equitable reward for performing it, which brings home directly to the operator that he has just as vested an interest in the prosperity of the firm as have the managers. This kind of relationship between effort and cash reward is best described as *task work*.

Task work specifies a relation between the whole task and the whole reward. More conventional schemes of wage payment make greater use of the cash motive, because, unlike task work, they leave some discretion to the operator to produce more bits of work for more pay, or less for less pay. The assumption with these schemes is that the operator, interested as he is believed to be in making more money – 'After all, that's what people come to work for, isn't it?' – will be moved to make it by producing more output. This is presumed to serve the manager's best interest, too, because he is getting more output from a given set of physical resources. So, whether the system of payment is a simple one which offers so much per piece, or a complicated one which includes rewards for quality, machine utilization and so on, the assumption is that the motive of cash reward is sufficient to move the operator to use the discretion given to him in directions desired by management towards higher output of high-quality parts. It is also expected that if the managers do not provide the proper tools and services to make possible the high earnings which the scheme promises, then the frustration of the worker at having to forgo the promised extra cash will lead him to put pressure upon the management to improve these tools and services. Therefore, in an indirect way, the cash motive of workers operating through a payment-by-results scheme can, it is said, keep continual pressure on management to improve.

The theory of task work and the theory of payment by results, while different in their application, are basically similar in according primacy to cash as a chief mover and in either neglecting or underestimating other motives. They also stress the directness of the relation of payment to results. The individual or the group (if the incentive is a group incentive) ought to see very quickly the reward for effort; otherwise the pulling power of extra cash is weakened. There are methods of payment by results which lay stress on the performance of a whole economic unit (such as a manufacturing plant). If employees of all kinds can be encouraged to appreciate that their continued employment and prosperity largely depend on the economic efficiency of the unit in question; if it can be shown that by using their knowledge and experience employees can contribute to the efficiency of the unit, i.e. the better use of resources; if the extra wealth created by their several contributions is available for sharing in ways that seem equitable to them, then they will be encouraged continually to seek or to suggest improvements and generally to offer their cooperation. This is the logic which underlies such schemes as the Scanlon Plan and the Rucker Plan,* and it is another expression of the idea that the prospect of economic reward can induce individuals to cooperate and to harness the detailed technical knowledge for the economic benefit of everyone and for the survival and growth of the unit.

Schemes of this type are usually administered jointly by employer and employees. Some measure of efficiency is agreed, e.g. value-added, volume/value of output, unit cost of production or ratios incorporating some of these. Improvements in the measures create a pool of extra wealth to be shared out in the proportions and at the intervals previously agreed. It has been argued in favour of such schemes that by encouraging cooperation at every level, which is usually done through small groups of operators and supervisors, they not only increase the income of the employee but

* For an account of such plans and their problems in practice, see Bowey (ed.) (1982).

they also encourage the employee's interest and participation in the affairs of the unit and in his or her own part of it, in that way improving job satisfaction and motivation to work. The practical difficulties lie in the fact that many of the influences on the performance of a unit are not wholly within the control of the employees – for example, the volume and value of output is determined in the market place, as are the costs of the raw materials used in the production process. Another problem is that employees might find it difficult to see how their own individual and group efforts are connected with the performance of the whole unit and the amount of bonus available. Unfavourable conditions in markets could well lead to losses in performance on some of the measures commonly used – value-added or volume of output, for example – which could mean that there is no bonus pool even though the effort has been made to use resources efficiently. When these things happen there is a loss of confidence in the schemes and motivation is adversely affected. Such schemes seem to work best with small units, where the link between behaviour and performance can be more easily seen.

One approach to a critique of the theory of payment by results is to ask what it is which is supposed to motivate managers. In most cases it is impossible to define clearly the task of the manager as a set of separable physical movements or clerical routines. In fact the skill of the manager is very largely a matter of solving non-routine, sometimes quite novel problems, in non-routine and novel ways. It is very difficult to break down his job into measured bits and to pay for the bits; and the total task is not easy to define or to relate to the salary. Yet managers are assumed to have, and the evidence is that they generally do have, a strong motive to do their jobs well and efficiently. They are expected to have an interest in the success of the organization as a whole and to see their job as a contribution; to a much greater extent than the operator, they do so. Managers will, of course, have ideas as to whether the money reward they receive is or is not an equitable reward for what they do, but it is not assumed that they will therefore do work exactly to correspond with the salary and no more. People behave in fact as if they can rely on managers to throw in their lot, as it were, with the organization. Managers will be moved, it is expected, to seek promotion and to work hard for it. Of course, firms pay cash bonuses to their managers, but these are seen as being due to the success of the organization as a whole to which all have contributed and not as a differential reward for a particular bit of effort. And bonuses usually come for managers after the effort has been put in and not as a result of a promise that they will be paid if certain defined tasks are satisfactorily carried out in a given time.

Perhaps an important motive of the manager is a general sense of obligation to the company he works for to do the best he can. In so far as the company prospers he will expect to share in that prosperity and to that extent cash is a strong motive. Yet whether his job be one of providing technical expertise or service, or taking part in making important decisions, or generally coordinating and facilitating the work of other men, it is likely to hold an absorbing interest for him.

What, then, is assumed to be the difference between a worker and a manager? Is it impossible that the worker will be unmoved by loyalty to the company, or that he can never be expected to see that his own prosperity is related to the prosperity of the company, unless this relationship is administratively transmuted into a direct and immediate equation which taps the acquisitive instinct? Is it also assumed that his job will inevitably be so unsatisfying in itself that the only way to overcome natural aversion is a bribe? Advocates of profit-sharing and the various schemes previously referred to which relate the economic rewards of everyone to the economic success of the company would answer: No. They would judge that the worker like the manager could be moved to his best efforts by a sense of obligation to the company that employs him, and that this would be encouraged by the feeling that he was sharing in an economic prosperity (and also perhaps a good name) which he had helped to shape.

The understanding we have gained so far from our studies of the social science of organization and management would suggest that, when choosing and designing in detail a system for paying wages and salaries, detailed account must be taken of the circumstances of the particular case. Like every other procedure aimed at the effective use of resources to provide a wanted good or service at an economic price, the payment system must be a 'good fit', taking into account markets, technology and the aspirations of employees who will be affected. This means that as those things change so must the design of the payment system. We would also expect that the power to influence changes of this kind will rarely be entirely in the hands of management. Other groups, with other aims and interests, might wish to have things done in ways that suit them.

Within this context, individuals seeking the satisfaction of their material needs and their needs to be well regarded by their fellows and to have satisfactory relationships with them, will try to influence their situation so that it provides these satisfactions. For the worker, whose individual discretion is by definition limited, but who works often in a group, the small group is the vehicle through which he seeks to influence his situation. The group itself may derive some of its power from, say, trade union backing, but it will use this in the context of the small group. Any attempt to exploit one motive, such as the money motive, and to frustrate others will lead to attempts to find other forms of expressing them. This, as we recall, goes some way to explain restriction of output. It also warns us that if a group is restricting output and it is thought necessary to stop it from doing so, it would not be enough merely to find another system of wage payment and put it in, on the assumption that the restriction must be necessarily caused by a fault in the design or administration of the incentive scheme. It might even lead us to ask whether it would be best to leave the group restricting output, since it would appear that unaided they have found ways to satisfy their needs by using their power to control the job, which management had not built into the formal organization. Social science would also lead us to make better guesses at what the outcome would be if it were decided to make changes. We would indicate which alternative to adopt. The range of human needs can be defined, and it can be asked whether the present working arrangement, system of wage payment and type of job, are contributing to these needs or not. It can also be asked to what extent those needs are being met by formal organization, to what extent they are being met informally, and at what cost to the organization. If the answers prove unsatisfactory, then one must search for alternatives which offer a balance between low cost and high social and individual satisfaction. It might be that any of the methods we have described for tapping motives, or any combination of them, may give satisfactory results in productivity and job satisfaction in a particular situation. The decision to adopt a particular method or not is a manager's job. A systematic procedure for choosing the payment system that best suits a particular set of circumstances has recently been published. The procedure is briefly outlined in Chapter 5 as an example of a practical application of a system theory of organization.

In recent years the interests of some social scientists have shifted away from relationships between managers and workers towards relationships between managers and managers, and between managers and the professionals that organizations employ. Technical progress and the growth of large-scale organizations have been largely responsible for this shift. Blake, for example, is almost exclusively concerned with management style and relations between managers. The same is true, but to a lesser extent, of Argyris and Likert. McGregor, in his advocacy of Theory Y, discusses the concept of management by objectives as an application of that theory. He is critical of those managers who have interpreted management by objectives as yet another opportunity to tighten direction and control, i.e. as merely a closer application of the theory of formal organization. McGregor proposes a version of management by objectives that emphasizes the link between managerial competence on the one hand and management job satisfaction and self-actualization on the other.

McGregor's version of 'Management by Objectives' (the invention of the name is attributed to Peter Drucker) has been taken up, developed and propagated by John Humble, the British management consultant (1969). Like the Blake grid, MBO is now widely known in British management and has been introduced by many firms.

MBO consists first in clarifying the definition of a subordinate's job as a result of open and frank discussion between superordinate and subordinate. This done, specific targets – jobs to be done within a specified time limit, for example – are agreed as reasonable aims for the subordinate and are recorded. Then, the superordinate manager must work hard to create conditions for the subordinate so that the latter will feel that he is being supported and encouraged rather than harried or controlled. In such a climate he will not only reach his targets but will exhibit growing confidence in his own ability to do bigger jobs with more difficult targets.

Finally, the results achieved by the subordinate in the pursuit of the agreed objectives are systematically appraised, and so is his general development as a manager. The appraisals may then be used to decide whether, for example, the subordinate needs further formal training, his present job needs enlarging, he is ready for greater responsibility, his salary and other rewards ought to be adjusted, he should be transferred horizontally, or even asked to leave.

The advantages claimed for MBO are:

1. That as a result of being involved in setting his own targets, and in defining his own job, the manager will be more highly motivated to improve performance.
2. That because targets are jointly set the superior gains a greater understanding of his subordinate's problems and is therefore better able to assess what changes are needed if these problems are to be minimized.
3. The data from target-setting and appraisal interviews are invaluable for identifying needs for training, education and personal and professional development generally.
4. The data for judging whether an individual is promotable or not are fuller and more systematically comparable under MBO and the criteria for doing so are the same for everyone. Justice is therefore done and seen to be done.

The McGregor–Humble version of management by objectives seems to me to be a rather loose amalgam of the older formal theory of organizations and the newer psychological doctrines. The two doctrines have this in common: they are universally prescriptive – that is, what they advocate is supposed to be good, whatever organization adopts it. MBO tacitly accepts the idea that all organizations are hierarchical in shape with authority distributed from the top down. Formal authority is also regarded as the main coordinating principle. The tasks of allocating work and the responsibility for getting work done and for coordinating it by authority *may* be done by strict definition from above, with control exercised by carrots and sticks of various kinds. However, the advocates of MBO see this kind of thing as constricting for the individual and therefore bad for the organization. They wish to create, within the positions as allocated by formal structure, high levels of commitment to company objectives, and a chance for individuals to develop their talents.

MBO is a doubly attractive doctrine. It accommodates within the same body of management practice the apparently opposing requirements for order, authority, discipline and continuity on the one hand (which emphasizes *constraints* on the individual), and democracy, participation, consultation on the other (which emphasizes *opportunities* for the individual). Because of this, management's authority at all levels is rendered legitimate, and so are the processes of advancement to positions of greater authority. The legitimacy arises from the fact that the main, and apparently contradictory, values of western culture are upheld and yet appear consistent. Our society also values advancement on merit, and this value is a strong point of MBO.

There is a plausibility and an attractiveness about MBO and the theories and prescriptions of, for example, Blake, Likert, Argyris and McGregor which we discussed earlier, which make criticism appear niggling. I have personally encountered unpopularity for presuming to offer criticism. However, managers should approach all prescriptions, whatever their origins sceptically and critically. The following are two of the many questions that they might ask:

1. Where is the evidence of a connection between the various prescriptions, e.g. 9/9 management, System 4, MBO on the one hand, and measured indicators of organizational performance on the other?
2. Are there any conditions, say, of technology, product, size, locality, in which an organization might perform well without MBO or 9/9 management, or whatever; or badly with them. If so, what are these conditions?

There is a small body of published knowledge about the outcomes of some applications of grid and T group training and a little about management by objectives (Wickens, 1968; Winn, 1969; Smith and Honour, 1969). However, there have been few attempts so far to relate the success or failure of such procedures to the nature of the situations to which they have been applied. It could be that certain styles of management might be appropriate and acceptable for some kinds of organization; other styles for others. This idea of best fit is now the subject of a growing body of research, which is referred to in detail in Chapter 5. This work is inconclusive as yet but in my belief it offers a wider, potentially more useful, perspective for the practising manager.

Technical and administrative change

Decisions to install new and labour-saving machinery, or to introduce new administrative systems of paper flow, or to add to existing plant, or to improve stock-holding facilities, or to introduce a new incentive scheme, or to install management by objectives, all involve a more or less complicated calculation of costs to be incurred against economic benefits to be gained. In the next chapter we shall refer briefly to the methods which economists have developed for improving the way these calculations are made. For the moment we confine ourself to the social and psychological consequences of the decisions.

It ought to be obvious that social and psychological reactions to the consequences of an economic decision could well give rise to costs which would make the project impractical. It seems often to be assumed that because, in the nature of things, these social and psychological reactions and their costs cannot be measured, they can safely be ignored or roughly guessed at. There are, in practice, three possible attitudes on the part of managers. *Firstly*, over-confidence that the benefits to be gained so outweigh the costs to be incurred that any cost outcome arising from social resistance will be easily covered; an example of this is the company which introduced a complicated incentive bonus scheme throughout its factory. Convinced that great gains in productivity would accrue, it gave generous pay guarantees to the trade unions in return for their cooperation. Shop-floor sabotage, additional costs of administration to counter the sabotage, and the cost of the guarantee wiped out the anticipated net advantage. *Secondly*, lack of awareness that there could possibly be any social costs. This might arise from taking a crude view that formal organization and money incentives properly organized will make mutual interest obvious. All that is needed then is a calculation of the costs of buying machinery, installing it, putting in an administrative system, and offering money rewards to employees for cooperation. The difficulty here might arise from delays in getting the machinery installed while arguments rage about who is to be transferred, and to which new job, and at what wages. In this case some of the costs have been anticipated; but not the cost of delay. The belief that formal planning would eliminate it makes anticipation unnecessary. *Thirdly*, because of lack of a means to anticipate the difficulties likely to arise, these difficulties are overestimated by management and the project is abandoned. In what way can the methods of social science help in anticipating the social and psychological consequences of technical and administrative innovation?

From what has been said so far we would expect that decisions to innovate would arise in response to a stimulus from the environment of the firm. The situation might call for the development of a new product, or an increase in the output of an old product, or a reduction in the cost of the product. This development in turn suggests technological or administrative improvements. The choice between the alternative technical and administrative means available will usually be made on economic grounds, and one factor in the calculation will obviously be the estimated time available to search for, and to examine the feasibility of, all possible solutions, and this puts a restriction on the number of alternatives considered. Once the decision is taken, it should then be possible to start a similar search for organizational alternatives, and it is in considering these alternative choices that some of the ideas we have been discussing come in useful.

We know that there is some relation between technology and the structure of organizations, and that if technology changes, the structure of the organization will most probably have to change, if the technology is to be efficiently exploited. But we also know that there is no exact correlation between technology and social structure, and that for any technology, or for that matter any administrative procedure, there may be a number of organizational alternatives. Our reference to the work of Burns earlier (page 57) also gave us the idea that mechanistic, rigidly defined structures were not likely to be effective in conditions of innovation. When we looked at the properties of social structure we learned to expect that the accretion of routine and custom which accompanies the development of social structures based on one technology, may obstruct the introduction of another. This inertia, it seems, is probably greater at the points where roles are highly programmed, and where this is accompanied by a high degree of social cohesion, usually at the bottom of the hierarchy. Finally, the inertia might be strengthened by external support for existing custom and practice through trade-union demarcation rules. Looking at the organization with these ideas in mind will show not only what organizational alternatives are possible but which of these will lead to the speediest and smoothest assimilation of the innovation. But more of this presently. Now we need to be reminded of what is meant by an organizational alternative.

Trist *et al.* in their study of mechanization in coalmines (1963) emphasized the general idea that although structural alternatives are limited by technology, they are by no means uniquely determined by technology. That is to say, there is scope for managers to discover what alternatives exist and to choose between them. In the coalmining example, there appeared to be a number of ways in which the total task of mechanized coal-getting could be divided up between teams on shifts and between the members of the teams. It also seemed possible to specify a number of ways of supervising and servicing the production processes. Such evidence as we have suggests that the same would apply to any task. For example, the division of labour and the supervisory structure for an electric arc steel furnace or a steel-rolling mill are not uniquely determined by the design of the machine. Nor does the design of a set of documents and a filing procedure completely limit how an office will be laid out and how the job in it will be defined, although it sets some limits. The idea of organizational choice is a great mental stimulus. It abjures technological determinism and raises the question 'If we have a choice, what are the criteria to be used in making it?' If the answer is that the criteria are satisfaction on economic, technical, social and psychological grounds, then just as each technical alternative was judged on its technical and economic merits, so each organizational alternative must be judged on its social and economic merits. Is it the most effective way to exploit the technical advantages of a process? Will it take a lot or a little time to introduce? What social and psychological resistance will it generate? What will be the long-term effects of this? We are now ready to seek methods of organizational diagnosis which will answer some of these questions.

Assume that a decision to innovate has been made and suppose also that several alternative methods of organization have been proposed. How are the likely consequences of adopting one or other of them to be judged? Knowledge of social science is useful in searching for answers. We know that each alternative is going to involve changes in role definition and in role relationships, and these are capable of specification. Then the question can be asked what groupings and individuals are going to be affected, and in what ways, and how are they likely to feel and to reason about it. To approach the same problem from a slightly different angle, we could say that our proposals for organization are directed to a restructuring of the social and technical environments of groups and individuals. The reactions of these people to this restructuring will be influenced very much by how much their interests, their expectations, their routines and their customs are going to be affected, much more on the basis of their personal circumstances than on consideration of what the change contributes to the organization as a whole. To estimate the impact of change it is necessary to know what is going to happen to groups and individuals, and what they are likely to do as a consequence. Change cannot be managed intelligently if one has only hazy knowledge and works with an assumption that people and groups will share the interests, routine and customs of all other people and groups and will react in the same way. Nor is it helpful to condemn them if they do not.

There are limits to the extent that any one group in an organization can have intimate knowledge of the expectations, interests, etc. of another, but this should not prevent the attempt to acquire such knowledge and to do so systematically. The formal and informal ways in which conflicts of interest and perspective are usually handled in the organization can also be discovered by careful investigation. We are arguing here for a diagnostic description of the organization as a system in equilibrium. We want to use this to predict the consequences of the disturbances which are bound to be caused by choosing and implementing one of the organizational alternatives.

All this raises problems of measurement. One can easily advance an objection against the argument of this chapter by saying that in practice the different outcomes of various action alternatives cannot easily be distinguished unless their probable impact can be measured with a reasonable degree of accuracy. This is admitted. Perhaps the only way to predict the impact is to attempt to measure the degree of acceptability of each alternative on the part of each affected group, or, more precisely, the acceptability of the measures proposed to deal with the issues raised for each group by each alternative. Therefore, if measurement is to be done, the things to be measured have to be defined, and this means that each alternative must be worked out in detail and steps specified by which they are to be implemented. Let us take an example. It is proposed that a new machine should be manned by five men. The process which is being replaced has twenty men working in groups of five. In the existing groups of five there is a hierarchy of skill and differential earnings. The alternative proposed is that the new team of five should comprise men of equal skill. The design of the new machine makes this possible and it seems desirable. If this alternative is adopted, fifteen men will have to be found new jobs or laid off. The decision will have to be made before this alternative is chosen rather than another. What principle is to be adopted to choose the five men from the twenty? The best of the four teams? The youngest five men? The best men from each team plus one other? Fire the lot and get a new team who can freshly learn the new process? Or what? And what wage is to be paid for the new job? Will the wage be halfway between that of a top and bottom crewman on the present process? How acceptable are these detailed plans likely to be to the people affected? Will they resent any attempt at planned redeployment? Or to abolish the differential? Will this raise issues of principle with the trade unions? If these detailed questions were asked about each issue arising for each group, and the results plotted on a scale, the lowest point of which indicates that the group is probably going to resist the proposed change entirely, and the highest that it will find the change quite acceptable, then there is a measure which will discriminate. If there is time and resources are available, detailed investigation and fine discrimination might be possible. If there is not enough time, a bigger risk is being taken, but in a real sense it will be a calculated risk.

It is entirely possible and likely that the most acceptable alternative on social grounds gives poor predicted results by technological and economic criteria. If one chooses an alternative which gives a better balanced result, the extent of the social problems to be faced will be clearly revealed. It can now be asked whether the existing mechanisms for redress of grievance are adequate and what else if anything needs to be done. Finally, it remains to assess the economic cost of adopting or not adopting the alternative which promises to maximize economic gain.

Enough has been said to show that the so-called intangibles and immeasurables can be identified, specified and roughly quantified, and that social and psychological problems can be intelligently anticipated if the analysis is carefully done.

Planning for change – socio-technical system approaches

The arguments of this chapter suggest some general injunctions to managers, to be followed when changes are contemplated.

1. Set up systematically and in detail the organization alternatives open.
2. Map out the present organization as a social system, not forgetting its external links.
3. List the groups affected by each organization alternative.
4. Examine the issues likely to be raised in each group from the adoption of each alternative.
5. Assess likely reactions on each issue and score for acceptability.

6. Test economic feasibility against social acceptability and adopt the course which offers the most adaptive and least costly balance.
7. Examine the problems this course raises and ask whether existing means of redress of grievance are adequate to cope. If not, take appropriate steps to create such machinery as seems to be required.

Managers who follow these injunctions will be less likely to experience surprising outcomes than those who do not. The likelihood can be further decreased if peers and subordinates are involved in the matter. The chapter concludes with an example of how the knowledge, experience and intelligence of people who play different roles in a work unit can be mobilized to map the unit as a sociotechnical system, and to plan a sequence of steps to achieve an agreed objective. The procedure to be followed is illustrated by reference to the planning of a change in a manufacturing system with productivity improvement in mind, but it needs little modification to make it applicable to any planned change.

In any given planned programme of productivity improvement, it is necessary to take four steps (Lupton and Tanner, 1981):

1. To define the unit of organization (a work-group, a manufacturing department or a plant, for example) whose productivity is to be improved and the productivity measure that is to be improved (output per man/hour, for instance).
2. To identify those items which, if they were changed, would have an effect on productivity (as defined) in the unit under consideration.
3. The sequence of change in the items which would have the maximum beneficial effect has to be determined, and this, as we shall see, is made up of a series of complex sub-steps.
4. To implement the changes decided upon. The process of making the first three steps, if properly handled, will greatly ease the problems of implementation.

If we suppose that the unit of analysis is a department of a manufacturing firm engaged in the final assembly of a complex engineering product, and the object is to improve output per man/hour, then Step 1, as we have defined it above, is complete. The boundaries of the unit have been defined and the objective set. We can now proceed to Step 2, which is to identify the items which, if changed, would affect the objective. It is absolutely essential at this stage that a representative of every activity in the unit should be involved including, if possible, the operators.

When confronted with a request to write a list of items which, if changed, would improve productivity, a personnel specialist might list operator selection and training, union attitudes and supervisory skills, while the department superintendent would probably include the quality of parts delivered to the department, the planning and control procedures and the effectiveness of maintenance. The maintenance engineer might mention the shortage of skilled fitters due to the company pay structure, and so on. There may be a reluctance to write exhaustive lists because people have usually formed strong views about what the significant items are. It is necessary to stress therefore at the outset of Step 2:

1. That every group concerned in the running of the department should be represented from the outset.
2. That each representative, separately at first, should draw up his own list of items, based on his experience, and missing out nothing which could possibly impinge on productivity.
3. That the lists are laid on the table at the first meeting of the group and are compared, and then compounded into a general list that everyone agrees is complete and comprehensive.

The following is a short list of items such as might emerge from such a process of comparison and discussion. We have found in practice that out of the process could come a list of anything from 50 to 80 items.

1. Quality of delivered components.
2. Procedures for recruiting operators.
3. Shift patterns.
4. Quality of fixtures.
5. Trade union demarcation rules.
6. Component stores procedures.
7. The system of wage payment.
8. The quality of first-line supervision.
9. The organization of maintenance.
10. Procedures for establishing work-standards.
11. Design of components.
12. Attitudes of operators.
13. Management style.

Those with experience of manufacturing systems will have no difficulty in adding some general items to this list, and there will of course be items which are specially relevant to a particular unit. It cannot be stressed too much, however, that there is no general list that will allow anybody to avoid the mental effort of compiling a list of their own, that the process (i.e. the meetings, the comparisons, the arguments) of drawing up the particular comprehensive list is as important as the outcome, and that no further work on the sub-steps of Step 2 must take place until the list is agreed by the group to be as exhaustive as they can possibly make it.

However, such lists are of limited use as they stand. The items are imprecise and there is as yet no way of deriving from them a systematic programme of change. To use the items further, we must add a little precision by asking the members of the group to take each item and to choose one or more dimensions to represent it.

For example, if we take the item 'the system of wage payment', we might represent it by two dimensions – complexity and equity, where complexity is defined by reference to the rules and procedures which determine the relationship of effort and reward, and equity by reference to the system's effectiveness in giving equal reward for equal effort to the individuals involved. The dimensions can be simply represented as five point scales for example:

Highly complex				Very simple
1	2	3	4	5

Highly equitable				Highly inequitable
1	2	3	4	5

The dimensions should *not* express values. It might seem, for example, that on the equity dimension it would be difficult to avoid concluding that an equitable system is always better than an inequitable one. But remember the objective in this case is to improve output per man/hour and not to design an equitable pay system. The equity of a pay system may or may not be strongly connected with output per man/hour. We do not have the same difficulty with complexity since we might agree that either simple or complex rules and procedures might, in association with a particular production system, be appropriate to achieve improved productivity.

It is better, therefore, when constructing dimensions for the items, to avoid 'value words' like good, fair, right, bad – unless they are defined carefully, as we have tried to do with 'equity' in the above example, so as to refer to some more objective, observable yardsticks like levels of pay and effort and their relationship.

The completion of this stage of the procedure gives a list of items each with a number of dimensions and this enables the planning group to address the questions, 'Where are we now on each of the dimensions in the unit under analysis?', and 'In which direction is it necessary to move on each of them if productivity, as defined, is to be improved?' The questions that now arise with respect to each dimension are:

1. Would a large movement along the dimension result in a small movement in productivity in the desired direction, or would a small movement lead to large changes? That is, how sensitive is the objective of improved productivity to movements of the items as measured on the dimensions.
2. How easy, or difficult, would it be to move along the dimension? We have called this aspect changeability.

The answers to the questions as agreed by members of the planning group can be indicated by ticks on scales showing degrees of *sensitivity* and *changeability*. It is clear that an item which is thought of as being highly sensitive might be very difficult to change, or vice versa.

The processes of defining dimensions, of positioning the unit in question on each of them, indicating the desired direction of

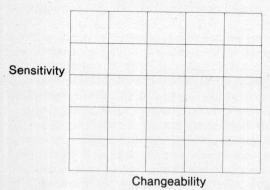

Sensitivity

Changeability

Table 2 5 × 5 sensitivity/changeability matrix

movement and scoring for sensitivity and changeability, are all expressions of the collective experience of the group in running the system. Arriving at a decision on where to position a cross, or an arrow, or a tick could involve long arguments illustrated by descriptions of the present and previous behaviour of the system. With each step each member of the team learns from his colleagues some aspect of the system he had only dimly perceived to be significant, and the group begins to share a working model of it in which technical, economic, social and psychological variables are included, and some of their relationships described.

It is helpful to draw a 5 × 5 blank matrix, and to transfer the results from the sensitivity–changeability procedure to the matrix.

We have now mapped the elements of the model of the unit into the two-dimensional space defined by sensitivity and changeability scales. This mapping helps us to consider which of the dimensions of our model should be included in the programme of change. Those which fall within the top right hand segment of the matrix are both highly sensitive and easily changeable. In other words, in the judgement of the group even small changes in these would bring great improvements in productivity and there are no significant obstacles to making such changes. Quite clearly they would be attractive candidates for inclusion in a programme of change. It is unlikely, however, that many items will fall into this area of the matrix if management has been doing its job. More commonly, they would be faced with a spread of items across the matrix from top left to bottom right. The choice which faces managers here is that between easily changed but relatively unrewarding items on the one hand, and highly rewarding but relatively unchangeable items on the other.

At this stage of the procedure it is necessary to decide whether to take the 'easy road' of changeable but increasingly unrewarding items, or the 'hard road' of increasingly difficult but highly rewarding items. The decision will hinge on such matters as whether the resources are available to attempt the difficult items or whether the motivational effects of successful change on a number of easy items make their pursuit worthwhile. We can, however, increase the power of our analysis to help with these decisions.

So far, we have treated the items to be changed as separate and distinct – but if we are dealing with a system, as we obviously are, then we must explore their interrelationships. This can be done by completing a 'cross-impact' matrix, as defined by the dimensions for the item. This ought ideally to be done by relating every item to every other item, but we illustrate it here by taking just 10 items.

The cross-impact matrix should be completed by each member of the group, after which comparisons can be made and reasons sought for similarities and differences. To fill in the matrix requires a judgement as to the strength of the influence of each item on every other. What we have to consider is the effect which a change (in a given direction) in one item will have upon the states of the other items in the system. This need not be a very precise measurement (although it could be) since a great deal of useful information can be generated through the cross-impact matrix even if we restrict the analysis to identifying whether effects are strong or weak, positive or negative. Positive effects are those which change the dependent item in the direction which is consistent with improving productivity; negative effects change items in an adverse direction.

When completed, the matrix enables one to identify those items which, if changed, would have wide repercussions, and those which are more influenced than influencing. We can illustrate this by examining the completed matrix (Table 3). We have deliberately used a simple scoring system for the sake of clarity; it gives ten points for a strong effect, one point for a weak effect and zero where no effect is expected. Positive and negative effects are indicated by a change of sign. The numbers indicate a set of items chosen on the basis of the sensitivity/changeability analysis to be part of a programme of change. The matrix yields up its information in the row and column totals. Each row records the effect which the item indicated has upon each of the other items, for example, the first row of the diagram shows the effects which item 1 has upon items 2–10. The row totals (positive and negative are kept separate) thus indicate the degree to which a change in a given factor affects the rest of the change programme. The higher the positive total, the greater the beneficial relationships within the programme. High negative row totals are indicative of internal conflicts between the items in the change programme. The cross-impact analysis offers us a means of identifying short cuts to the completion of the programmes. If we change item 4 in our example, we change items 1, 2, 7 and 8 in a major way as well. We can see this by considering the major effects in the appropriate row for the matrix. Note that there is only a very small negative outcome (factor 9), which we can ignore. These changes, in turn, will have

Dimension	1	2	3	4	5	6	7	8	9	10	+	−
1	✕	10	10	0	-1	1	0	1	0	0	22	1
2	10	✕	10	0	10	1	0	10	0	0	41	0
3	10	10	✕	0	0	0	1	1	0	0	23	0
4	10	10	1	✕	1	1	10	10	-1	0	43	1
5	-1	-10	0	0	✕	10	1	1	-1	0	12	12
6	1	0	1	0	0	✕	1	10	0	0	13	0
7	0	0	0	0	0	0	✕	1	-1	0	1	1
8	-1	0	0	0	0	1	-1	✕	0	0	1	2
9	0	0	-1	-10	0	0	-10	1	✕	10	11	21
10	0	0	0	0	0	0	0	0	0	✕	0	0
+	31	30	22	0	11	15	13	35	0	10		
−	2	10	1	10	1	0	11	0	3	0		

Table 3 Example of a cross-impact matrix

further effects. The first change will lead to a chain reaction whose
path we are able to plot through the matrix. For this example we
can look at the rows for items 1, 2, 7 and 8. We can see that we
get a positive additional effect on items 3 and 5. Therefore a change
in item 4 could eventually lead to major advantageous changes in
items 1, 2, 7, 8, 3 (via 1) and 5 (via 2). Only items 9 and 10 would
have to be pursued independently.

The column totals record the degree to which the given items
are expected to be influenced by the other items in the programme.
High scores indicate that the items are very likely to be changed
by other elements of the programme. Low scores indicate that they
will not be subject to such changes. Item 4 has a low column score –
this is one of the reasons why it was chosen to start the change
sequence above; item 9 also has a low column score and it too
would be directly changed (bringing about the completion of the
programme through its influence upon item 10).

The cross-impact analysis can be taken a stage further. In the
first part of our procedure we assessed the changeability and sensitivity of each item. These scores can now be used to weight the
cross-impact matrix. For example, if we multiply each column of
the matrix by the sensitivity score of the respective item, the row
totals reveal not only the inter-connectedness of the change programme, but also the probable relative contribution to productivity
of changes in particular items.

By this time a list of items to be changed, with hope of great improvement (sometimes without great effort) in productivity, can be drawn up. One also knows by this time, having done the cross-impact analysis, what the process of change for the better will look like, as a matter of organization dynamics. One has also identified the nature of the possible obstacles.

Finally, the change programme can be planned and implemented as a set of sequential steps. But now one has to ask questions like: Who has to be changed, and how? Some of those questions will have already been answered during the process of evolving the change programme, for example in scoring for changeability and in the evolution of common models and lists of items for change. We stress that the more people likely to be affected by a process of change who have been involved in the procedure we have just described, the better for the smoothness of its implementation. In addition, everyone learns more, during this process, about what makes their organization work effectively, which is a very practical justification for wide participation in decisions about change.

5
Organization Theory and
its Practical Uses

By simplifying the categories of Mintzberg and Boyatzis, we may say that managers have three main roles: they act as social engineers, organizational clinicians and leaders. In their role as *social engineers*, their task is to create and continuously to maintain the arrangements for the efficient and effective production of goods and services. This involves, amongst other things, the design of formal organizational procedures, the deployment of people into jobs, and the inducement of those people to work together efficiently towards agreed objectives. As *clinicians*, by explicit or intuitive diagnosis, managers identify the causes of the malfunctioning of organizations or their component parts, and decide what has to be done to correct them. They also practise *leadership*, that is they persuade people of the rightness of the courses of action they have chosen, and work to win their willing cooperation for implementing them, not only by precept but also by example.

As *social engineers* managers seek technical procedures. As *clinicians* they need models of the structure and functions of organizations to refer to (just as doctors need models of the structure and functioning of human organisms), and questions to ask which will reveal the patterns of causation behind the symptoms of malfunctioning. As *leaders* they need knowledge of subordinates, their capacities and potential, and the setting in which they work.

There has been no lack of providers of technical aids to the manager in his role as social engineer. Some of these, for example the Blake grid and Management by Objectives, have already been mentioned and briefly discussed. In organizational design we have also encountered the injunctions of classical theory, and the powerful apparatus of scientific management, including techniques of method-improvement work measurement, shop layouts for efficient work flow, and work measurement techniques. In the realm of payment systems there exist procedures for designing and installing, as well as maintaining, such pieces of social technology as the Scanlon and Rucker plans. The technologies of job evaluation are also very well developed. More recently, European managers have become interested in an item of organizational technology, reputedly invented in the USA but developed into a popular and well-articulated system in Japan, namely the quality control circle which involves groups of workers in the management process as discoverers of new and improved methods (*Q C Circle Activities*, Ishikawa (ed.) 1958). There are of course techniques of production control, budgetary control and the like which are, in the last resort, devoted to controlling the behaviour of people for organizational purposes: where they must work, how they must work, how much money they are allowed to spend, and so on. In fact, the manager as social engineer is an avid searcher after well-developed procedures to enable him to work effectively and more professionally, and to control the work of others. As decision-makers, many managers have been attracted to the methods evolved by the US consultants Kepner and Tregoe (1973). These methods are designed to teach managers how to proceed rationally – to set objectives, to gather facts, to propose and evaluate courses of action and to decide on the best course and implement it. The procedure I have devised with my colleague Ian Tanner (outlined above, pp. 114–22) for planning organizational change is a procedure of the same kind, although putting perhaps more emphasis on group processes as mechanisms for eliciting the experience of group members and using those processes to generate commitment to jointly defined aims. In brief then, the manager has much social and psychological technology to call upon. His problem is to decide whether the tools available are well matched to the job in hand, and there is no simple technology for solving that problem. Theory could be a help.

Sociologists and social psychologists, for reasons discussed earlier (page 76), have never been prolific providers of technical procedures for managers, unless action research, organizational development, etc. are so defined. They have, however, been the main providers of models and methods for the clinical process; theorizing and testing theory against the facts have been their main preoccupation. Managers, of course, have their own theories which have evolved from their own experience. The value of the social scientists' theories to the manager is to give him more general and objective reference points, and to indicate how his implicit theoretical ideas may be made explicit. Explicit theory is a useful aid to learning. With explicit theory one knows why one is doing what one has decided to do. If the outcomes are not as one anticipated, then one can raise doubts about the theory. This should lead to its modification so that it becomes a better explainer and predictor. Just as importantly, it makes possible the reasoned critique of social engineering techniques and encourages the manager to develop social technology direct from the theory and not to rely on others to do this; which is at once more economical and more satisfying. Explicit theory also makes accurate diagnosis possible and facilitates the explanation to others of why particular courses of action have been chosen to resolve problems.

It goes without saying, I believe, that without a deep knowledge of the springs of human behaviour and of the settings which surround it, leadership as we have defined it will be ineffective. Leadership style is affected by time, place, task and setting, and social science has helped define the nature of the connection and its relation to performance (Vroom and Yetton, 1971).

One purpose of this final chapter is to describe some cross-disciplinary developments in the theory of organization and management in the expectation that they will open up new ways of thinking about the problems of management. However, its main aim is to exemplify the process whereby useful technical procedures for managers can be derived from theory. The examples are drawn from two separate but related strands in organization theory which we know about already from previous chapters. The first of these strands is the contingency theory of organization originating with Joan Woodward and Tom Burns and carried forward by Lawrence and Lorsch, to whose work we will refer. The second strand of development is the socio-technical systems theory associated with the Tavistock Institute and the Department of Social Anthropology at Manchester University. From the contingency theory of organizations we shall derive a procedure for arriving at an appropriate pattern of specialization and coordination for an organization; and from the socio-technical systems approaches we evolve procedures for choosing a payment system, and for reconciling economic, technical and human considerations in the design of a manufacturing system.

We have already referred to the theory of the organization as a socio-technical system with economic tasks. It will not have escaped the alert reader that this and other parts of the social science of organizations have emerged more from a desire to explain the social and psychological obstacles to getting economic things done than with the processes of deciding what economic things should be done. The understanding of the obstacles is of course important to those decisions and an economic theory of the organization should include them, but just as sociologists and social psychologists have tended to neglect the economic and political variables in their theories, so economists have given little methodical attention to the social, psychological and political variables. A theory that attempts to encompass all the variables should therefore be a welcome addition to the intellectual tool-kit of the manager – we therefore begin by reviewing the work of Cyert and March.

The behavioural theory of the firm

As Cyert and March point out (1963), the economists' theory of the firm is 'primarily a theory of markets ... [it] purports to explain at a general level the way resources are allocated by a price system'. The theory, they say, was never intended to answer questions about how resources are allocated *within* the firm, nor to explain the social processes by which decisions about prices, outputs and marketing policies are made. They themselves have attempted a theory which answers these questions. They draw heavily on some of the sociological theories of organization to which we have already referred, and to earlier work by March and Simon (1958) on more general processes of decision making in organizations. The theory, it should be added, owes much to investigations of actual processes of decision making.

To the practising manager, the idea that decisions made in organizations about prices and output and budgets are partly the outcome of the problems posed by the economic environment, partly the result of the way various groups and individuals interpret these problems and attempt to influence the processes of decision making, will not appear to be novel. Cyert and March have merely taken the idea and have tried to spell out the influences which play upon those who are interpreting the problems posed by the environment and the processes which lead to decisions being taken to deal with them.

A common idea of organization amongst managers, which is partly due to economic theory and partly due to the theory of formal organization, describes organization in terms of activities rationally assigned and coordinated to make possible the achievement of an economic objective which is itself a rational response to market forces. Cyert and March prefer the sociologists' model, in which the division of labour required by technology and the scale of operations gives rise to sub-units specialized by task and function, in which the power to influence events is differentially distributed. In this model there is no single rational economic objective; the system of administrative control is not unitary. The organization might well have a number of general goals which might not be consistent with one another. There will be a tendency for sub-units to develop their own goals, which again may be inconsistent with one another and with the organizational goals. On this view, in order to predict what decisions will be made about economic quantities, one would need to know not just that there are economic pressures from the environment. One would ask also: Which information about what parts of the environment reaches what parts of the organization? How does this information affect the aspirations, expectation and goals of the sub-units, and how does this in turn influence the political process of deciding what to do? It is not difficult to see the practical potentialities of this sort of theorizing. It encourages straight thinking about the way organizations work and is obviously leading towards a more comprehensive view of their structure and functioning. Surely, if the manager, as a result of his appreciation of such a comprehensive theory comes to know more about what we may describe as the anatomy and physiology of organization, then he will move more intelligently and confidently in his job. Let us look briefly at the outlines of Cyert and March's theory to see whether these remarks seem to be justified.

What do we need to know if we wish to predict which goals (policies) an organization will decide to pursue in relation, for example, to market shares, output levels and product pricing? We should clearly want to investigate the structure to see which sub-units are involved in what Cyert and March refer to as the coalition which decides these things and what their own interests and aims are. We should want to examine the customary processes of bargaining, politicking and rational problem-solving which characterize the coalition. In addition, the structure of power and influence in relation to particular goals and policies would be of concern to us. It would not be enough to say that the organization has certain kinds of problems posed by its environment. We should rather ask what it is about the situation facing the organization which is seen to be problematical, by whom and why. Pushing further, we would inquire about the way information is sought and given about what goes on inside and outside the organization and how the expectations of groups and sub-units are affected. Knowing what we do about organizations, we should also expect that there would be established routines for solving some kinds of recurrent problems and for regulating the flow of information, and we should want to know what these were.

But a theory has to be more than just a check-list of questions and categories of answers. There must be some way of describing analytically the relations between the factors covered in the questioning. All our questions so far (which are only a small part of the range discussed by Cyert and March) have assumed that there is going to be conflict and uncertainty in the decision-making process. The organization implied in these questions is ridden with risk and uncertainty and is conflict-generating. One has to agree, I am sure, that organizations *have* problems of resolving internal conflict and of coping with the uncertainties of markets, supplies and governments' policies. These could be described as centrifugal tendencies. Yet it is also an observed fact that organizations cohere and survive. So there must be centripetal tendencies at work too. Cyert and March argue, from the empirical evidence, that conflict is always latent in organizations. Whether it remains so depends upon the operation of certain social and administrative mechanisms. Amongst these are the delegation of problem solving, which means that sub-units and individuals solve limited, defined problems, in what they see as rational ways. Any inconsistency with others' solutions to other limited problems is not clearly perceived. Decentralization of the authority to make the rules governing decision taking is also conflict-avoiding, provided that the rules are generally acceptable. Finally, the organization tends to take in sequence and not in parallel the consideration of goals or policies which are likely to conflict.

As to uncertainty, the further one peers into the future the more vague and uncertain that future becomes. This applies to organizations as well as to individuals. Therefore, organizations tend to the kind of forward planning which eschews long-term prediction and promises short-term control. This means that organizations usually attend to pressing problems as they arise and at the same time try to structure the environment (by pacts with competitors and suppliers, for example) to minimize long-term uncertainty.

The empirical evidence suggests to Cyert and March that organizations rarely look at the complexities of their environment with a view to understanding them. Nor do they merely pick up random information. The information-gathering process seems to start with the appearance of what is conceived by the organization, or by part of it, as a problem. Then the simplest possible explanation of why the problem has arisen is proposed and this forms the basis of information seeking and decision making, until it is shown that something more complicated is needed as a matter of practical necessity. It seems to Cyert and March as if this process of economy in explanation, added to the previously mentioned breaking down of complex problems into simple ones, and the acceptance of decision rules, ensures some consistency of goals and helps to keep down the amount of conflict and uncertainty.

Obviously Cyert and March are attracted by the resemblance of an organization to a living organism, with its power to adapt to a changing environment through its reactions to the stresses and strains generated by conflict and uncertainty. It is claimed, persuasively, that organizations, like individuals, have the power to learn from experience how to survive. They learn how to change their goals, how to revise procedures and rules, how to look for and to find new and significant information. To be sure, they do this through the agency of people, but, as we have seen, individuals are under strong influence to behave according to the roles defined for them.

Socio-technical approaches

Working largely independently, research workers at the Tavistock Institute have gone further than most in building a framework which can bind together the various psychological and sociological theories of organizations. In his book *The Enterprise and its Environment*, Rice, a member of the Tavistock group, elaborates a conceptual framework which, as he says, 'relates individuals, groups, and institutions to each other in one coherent system' (1963, page 10). What follows is a free summary of Rice's account.

The framework proposed exhibits the organization as a series of encapsulated significant environments.* The individual member of an organization has his internal world and an external world, which

* My term – T.L.

importantly includes the other individuals with whom he constantly interacts on the job. This working group is a significant environment for the individual, in which he seeks satisfactory relationships. The group too has its own internal life, which comprises the complex of interpersonal relations, influenced by shared or discrepant norms of behaviour, common or conflicting beliefs and attitudes. It has its own external environment composed of adjacent groups and individuals. A sub-unit of a large organization might include many such groups, and its internal system is described by the relationships between them. Its environment consists of other sub-units and the organization as a whole. The organization, i.e. the whole complex of interrelated and encapsulated sub-units, groups and individuals, has to adapt to a changing world which includes other groups and organizations such as shareholders, customers, trade unions and governments.

The internal life of an organization is characterized by transactions across the boundaries of groups and sub-groups by individuals who manage the relationships between the groups and their several environments. As we know from our previous analysis, the division of labour, which is created to achieve what Rice calls the primary task* of the organization, helps shape the structure of sub-units and groupings and allocates to them their specific primary task. We have also had occasion to note that the effective pursuit by one group of its task might bring it into conflict with another.† We also know that the interrelations between individuals, groups and sub-units give rise to customary ways of doing things which are not officially prescribed and to equally unofficial transactions, all in the process of adjusting and adapting to the demands of the environment.

To Rice, as to the economist, an organization is an open system. It takes in inputs from the environment, converts them, and sends outputs back into the environment. His operating systems, i.e. the sub-units to which we have referred, either deal with inputs or outputs, or carry out processes of conversion. Of course each operating system has its own input–conversion–output procedure. The management of the organization is made up of those *general managers* who stand at the boundary of the whole system and its environment, the *operating managers* who stand at the boundary

---

* i.e. the task which has to be performed if the organization is to survive.
† For example, in Gouldner's study of succession.

of the operating systems, and the *managers of the control and service functions* who stand inside the boundary and whose job it is to integrate the various operating systems so that they serve the overall primary task of the organization.

The concept of *system*, crucial to this theory of organization, has not yet been defined. *System* expresses the idea of a set of parts related to each other in patterns (or configurations) which mark them off from other systems with different patterns. The idea of a system also entails the idea of a boundary, an environment and equilibrating mechanisms. These mechanisms are set in motion when changes take place in the environment which affect one or other parts of the system and which induce stresses which must be relieved by a reordering of the parts. We have described an organization as a series of systems within systems. We now add the concept of mechanisms of adjustment and realignment which will be set in motion by changes in the environment.

The organization, with its sub-systems, groups and individuals, does not react automatically in its environment. The processes through which equilibrium is sought result from conscious decisions and activities of individuals and groups. Someone has to decide what changes have to be made in response to environmental stimuli, whether to diversify products, to purchase a new machine, to employ a personnel manager. Someone has to define new tasks and create new organizational configurations. The successful adaptation of the system will depend partly on these decisions, but not wholly. The organizational strategy might run counter to the smooth adaptation of a sub-group to *its* environment and then there will be resistance to change. Or the strategic decision itself might be ill-suited to the wider environment, because of pressures from inside the system. It is because organizations do not have built-in automatic mechanisms of adaptation such as animals have, nor mechanical systems of feedback and control such as an engine governor has,* that the practice of management is of such great importance, and so are the administrative procedures which provide information and cues to set in motion processes of adaptation. This is why new sciences like cybernetics are important to management, because in one aspect an organization is a system of information flows. Computers are also invaluable as part of a more

---

* Although some administration procedures incorporate quasi-mechanical feedback, the stock-control system mentioned earlier is one example.

efficient system of information feedback. But, as March and Simon point out, even with all these aids the central nervous system of the human organization is still an extremely crude mechanism. Although the acceleration of technical advance in information transmission should add much refinement to the capacity of organizations to respond to changes in their environment and to plan and control internal processes more effectively, the *choice* of modes of response, the preparation of plans and the processes of control, will probably demand more, rather than less, from human beings.

Organization and environment

The models I have just described show great promise of practical implementation. Recent studies using open-system concepts are branching radically away from the still prevalent preoccupation with universal prescriptions for management decision. Organization theory is demonstrating an increasing capacity to spawn organization technologies.

There is a discernible trend for some branches of organization theory, particularly those most affected by the open-system perspective, to eschew universal prescriptions. To be sure, there are still those who continue the search for such prescriptions and some of these were referred to earlier. The alternative, or rather one possible alternative, to the search for universal prescriptions is to pursue what might be described as the definition of best fit.

When we discussed earlier the work of Woodward (1959, 1965), Burns and Stalker (1961), Pugh *et al.* (1963) and Lupton (1963), we noted their concern with the differences rather than the similarities between organizations, with reference to the expedients the organizations severally adopt to cope successfully with the problems posed by their particular environments. Woodward, for example, suggested a relationship between technology, the structure of organization and performance, and Burns and Stalker discussed a connection between the rate of environmental change, the tightness or looseness of managerial structure, and organizational performance. Pugh and his colleagues have been devising ways of measuring and profiling the many structural characteristics of organizations. This makes it possible to distinguish one organization from another with great precision, in ways similar to those used by psychologists when they distinguish individuals by profiling their many personal characteristics. Pugh and his colleagues are also seeking ways to define and measure the characteristics of the environment of organizations. One of their objectives in doing so is to explain what characteristics of organization when matched with what characteristics of environment are conducive to high organization performance, and what modes of group and individual behaviour are associated with such characteristics. Lupton (1963), Cunnison (1965) and Wilson (1962) have traced relationships between the differing environmental characteristics of organizations and the observed differences in behaviour of workers.

The distinction between what might be called the universalists and the relativists in organization theory is worth spending a little more time on because of its present and potential practical relevance. It is of great practical significance whether one kind of managerial style or procedure for arriving at decisions or one kind of organizational structure is suitable for all organizations, or whether the managers in each organization have to find the expedient that will best meet the particular circumstances of size, technology, product, competitive situation and so on. In practice managers do, indeed must, attempt to define the particular circumstances of the unit they manage, and to devise ways of dealing with these circumstances. I have often observed that their success in doing so is limited by their belief that there must be a universal prescription. This belief can obscure some of the possibilities that are open. Managers acting in this way may fail to develop criteria for choosing the alternative which is best suited to the particular circumstance from those that are available.

This is not to suggest that there are never alternatives that are universally applicable, nor that having defined the circumstances some generally available solution might do. There may be such alternatives, but the research evidence strongly suggests that because organizations have problems of adapting to their environments, and that since the environments differ and are always changing, whether slowly or quickly, then the observer might expect to find that the expedients that lead to successful adaptation will differ from organization to organization.

Given that the expedients appropriate to a particular environment could be precisely defined, then managers would have a very powerful tool in their hands. For example, if it were possible to find ways of measuring the characteristics of an organization's environment, of defining the range of alternative structures, systems of control, etc. that could cope with that environment, and a procedure for choosing from amongst them the one that is the best fit, some of the uncertainty in managerial decision making would be removed.

Social scientists are a long way from the time when they will be able to tell the manager *exactly* how to match his organization structure to technology, size and competitive position; how to choose an appropriate payment system for workers or a salary structure for managers; or how to manipulate the environment so as to reduce labour turnover; but there are three recent researches dealing with some of these matters that are very encouraging. I shall describe briefly the findings of these researches and indicate how I see them influencing the processes of managerial decision. The approach of the three researchers in question has been very much influenced by the systems view of organization, which was described earlier when discussing the work of Cyert and March, and Rice. It also incorporates the findings of relativists like Woodward, and Burns and Stalker. Further, the research reported is not inhibited by the boundaries of academic disciplines.

I refer first to the work of Lawrence and Lorsch: *Organization and Environment* (1967) reports the results of a research project, and is not greatly concerned to examine the relevance of their findings for managerial decision. However, for my courses at the Manchester Business School I have been able to derive from the ideas of Lawrence and Lorsch the outline of a practical procedure for designing or redesigning an organizational structure.

Lawrence and Lorsch conceive of organizations (at least manufacturing organizations) as having environments that might be conveniently thought of as being divided into three segments, a market segment, a research and development segment and a technological segment. Each of these environments is likely to have different rates of change, and each of them is likely to differ also in the length of time that elapses between a decision being made, or an action taken, and the consequences of that decision or action becoming known to the one who made it and to those who will judge his performance. For example, the rate of change in the field of knowledge that is explored by an R and D department may be very high, while, at the same time and in the same organization, the rate of change in customers' tastes or competitors' tactics might be low, and the rate of change of product or method very low. The fundamental research scientist in a research laboratory of an organization might not find out for years what use, if any, the organization made of his findings and whether economic benefit accrued, but the feedback of complaint or praise from customers to the marketing man may be very fast, and faster still may be the verdict on the quantity and quality of the output of a process or a production department. Plainly, the rates of change and time-spans of feedback will differ from organization to organization as well as from segment to segment in the same organization. The market for motor cars differs from the market for chocolate, as do the technology, and the research and development requirements. So, argue Lawrence and Lorsch, the requirement for specialization will probably differ in an organization making chocolate from that in an organization making motor cars.

Imagine a number of organizations of the same size, making a similar product for a similar market using similar methods. Each would respond to the imperatives of market and technology by devising what seemed an appropriate division of labour amongst managers and professional specialists. That is to say, its directors and senior managers would ask themselves questions about the best way to divide up the tasks of the organization as they see them: Should we have central divisions each comprising different kinds of specialists – purchasing men, marketing men, production men, personnel men – or should we group the specialist around his managers at a lower-level cost or product centre? These might be among the questions they would ask. Behind them is another: If we allocate the tasks posed by the environment in this way or that way so as to make the best use of our specialists, what problems of subsequent coordination will we create?

I am not suggesting, of course, that on a given date in the history of a company senior managers sit down and pose questions like this and then try to think up once-and-for-all answers. The process by which a given organization's structure emerges is a gradual one, a succession of responses to environmental stimuli, or internal processes of accommodation; although periodically fairly drastic changes may be made. What I *am* suggesting is that similar organizations with their similar environments might emerge at the end of the process with different procedures for allocating tasks amongst specialists and coordinating their activities thereafter. Clearly there can be no unique solution to the problems of organization that are posed by similar environments. It is possible, however, that some of the possible solutions are likely to be more successful than others, successful in the sense that the organization adapts to its environment with a high degree of success.

If this view of things be accepted we could seek ways to put similar firms in rank order of their performance on a number of measures of success, and then examine the structural expedients that they have adopted to cope with their (similar) environments. This would enable us to discern the range of expedients which seem to posit successful performance. We can do better than that, however; we can use the research findings of social scientists to arrive at informed guesses (before we systematically compare the similar firms) as to what will be the organization structure and patterns of behaviour of the successful ones. This is a good way to test the theory, and Lawrence and Lorsch have done it.

If the research and development task is to be performed effectively, in conditions where the rate of growth and transmission of new knowledge is fast and the environment uncertain, and the time-span of feedback is lengthy, then previous research would suggest that a loosely structured organization, with an egalitarian democratic ethos and a high degree of personal discretion, would be appropriate. If all the segments of the organization have the same rate of change and time-span of feedback then it would follow that the procedures for coordination between organization segments would not be onerous, and would differ from those required where the various environments differed with respect to the characteristics already mentioned. Cyert and March deal with this kind of problem when they speak of the multiple objectives of the organization and the expedients used to avoid the worst consequences of environmental and organizational segmentation. Lawrence and Lorsch are more concerned to speculate about the structural prerequisites for adaptive integration and hence high performance, given the structure of specialized activities adopted.

For example, one finds in organizations people or departments whose job arises from the need to coordinate the activities of other people and departments, rather than as a direct response to the imperative of the environment. These people and departments are expected to see, for example, that conflicts about access to resources, or misunderstandings arising from professional jealousies or lack of information, do not obscure and frustrate the processes of adaptation at the level of the organization as a whole. Has the research on organization anything to say about the characteristics of the effective integrator? Yes, it has; and Lawrence and

Lorsch have derived from it seven partial determinants of effective integration. They refer *inter alia* to the location of the integrator in relation to the integrated; how, and for what, the organization rewards him; what competences he, or they, have; and what modes of conflict-resolution are used.

A contingent procedure for organization design

Compared with the practical injunctions of the early theorists of formal organization (referred to on page 34) the ideas emerging from the work of Lawrence and Lorsch are very complex. Indeed any theory about design which rests on the principle 'it all depends' is bound to be more complex than one which rests on supposedly universally applicable injunctions. To accept a 'contingent' theory as a practical guide is to face the challenge of identifying and measuring the contingent factors. In engineering or architectural design that is readily accepted. The designer is always seeking for combinations of the materials available to him which will match as nearly as possible the design objective – for example, an aeroplane to fly at high altitudes at supersonic speeds, or a building to serve as an electronics factory. It is perhaps surprising that it was ever thought that all organizations should be structured according to the same general principles rather than be designed for a particular purpose and a particular context. A 'contingent' theory of organization enjoins the designer to seek a general *procedure* for arriving at a particular design, rather than a set of general principles to apply to every design. It is possible to derive the outline and source of the details of such a procedure from the ideas of Lawrence and Lorsch and other 'contingency theorists'.

Let us begin with the simple idea that all employing organizations share one general characteristic: they all procure inputs and transform them into outputs which are then, as goods and services, disposed of at a price to consumers or clients. In a manufacturing organization, for example, raw materials, components, and services like water and electricity are purchased from other organizations. The purchaser in this case is the customer of these other organizations, paying a price for *their* outputs. Our organization also recruits from the labour market and the wages and salaries paid are analogous to the price paid for other inputs. The organization might also spend money in order to gain access to technical know-how, by purchasing a licence to make certain kinds of products or to use certain kinds of technology, for example – many organizations from all over the world have purchased the right to make plate glass by the float process invented by Pilkington Brothers, a British firm. Know-how may also be imported by the employment of scientists and technologists who search the world of science and technology for new ideas which can be developed to become new products or new technologies. It is to be expected that our company will employ some specialists who will make sure that the price, quality and delivery times of raw materials and components are according to specification; others who will recruit people with appropriate skills and qualities and who will see that they are appropriately trained to carry out specialized tasks; and yet others who know where to look for scientific and technical knowledge and have the ability to turn it to the advantage of the organization in the shape of new products and processes. If our organization is a medium-sized or large organization, the specialized activities of procuring inputs will become specialized departments – for example a purchasing department, a personnel and industrial relations department, and a research and development department. In a very large organization with a complex input environment, there may be several specialized sub-departments dealing with different sub-environments, one to deal with those essential raw materials which tend to fluctuate widely in price and are regulated through futures markets (like copper, for example), another for components of high technical specification, and so on. The personnel department may be subdivided into specialist areas of operator recruitment and training, management recruitment and development, top management succession planning, industrial relations, and personnel research. Research and development could spawn specialist areas in fundamental research, new product development, new process development, and trouble-shooting on products and processes which are beyond the development stage. In a very small organization, of course, the proprietor might do all these things himself.

If we turn now to that part of the organization which disposes of its output at a price, we again find a need for specialists. Certainly, people are needed whose job it is to find clients and to discover what they need and what they want. Others will be expected to know who the competitors are, who their clients are, and what prices they are charging. Other specialists will be employed to persuade people to buy the product or service, and yet others to actually sell it at the point where deals are done. In the case of complex engineering products which have to be installed on the buyer's premises, say a computer or a complex machine-tool, one may find another group of specialists whose work it is to commission the product. Further types of specialists could be those with responsibility for marketing and selling one of many products; those who are expert in advertising or market-research; and those who distribute the product or arrange for its distribution. Already we see that if our organization were to examine those parts of its 'boundary' which touch particular suppliers, particular customers, or particular sources of know-how, and for each of them ask which would be the most appropriate specialists to employ, and how they could be organized into departments according to the size of the task involved in dealing effectively with their 'segment' of the environment, it would be possible to arrive at a structure of 'requisite specialization', for procuring inputs and disposing of outputs efficiently. The emerging structure could include:

1. A purchasing department, subdivided into raw material procurement, and components purchasing.
2. A personnel department, subdivided into personnel research, operator recruitment and training, management recruitment and development, overseas postings, industrial relations.
3. A research and development department, comprising new product development, new manufacturing system development, plant commissioning.
4. A sales and marketing department, comprising market research, advertising, media research, sales for product group (a) and product group (b).

Depending on the particular nature of its environment the list emerging from another organization might be quite different. Decisions about the appropriate *nature* and *structure* of specialized activities might be influenced by projections about the future, as well as by present circumstances. What *is* decided will be by reference to effective performance, the measures of which will also be contingent. For example, effectiveness in raw material procurement might be measured comparatively, i.e. how much better or worse we are than our main competitors in getting good materials at a keen price and with prompt and/or predictable delivery. In selling and marketing this might be measured by trends in the volume and value of finished products delivered to the market in particular periods.

We have covered some possible aspects of the input and output environments of a particular company, but these are not the only environments that modern organizations have to adapt to. There is much modern legislation which can affect a company, and large companies, especially, will wish to influence the legislators not to pass laws which are damaging to them, or which are perceived to be potentially so. There are also public pressure groups – the conservationists, the anti-nuclear lobby, and so on – whose activities might affect some companies adversely. The general image that the company enjoys with the public might also affect its sales and its ability to recruit people, and that has to be attended to by employing specialists and/or special departments to deal with governments and pressure groups. Companies must also have access to credit in order to finance investment and stocks.

Already there is a formidable list of different specialist departments which are required by our company if it is to influence or respond appropriately to its environment, and we have not yet mentioned the specialist areas which might emerge contingently in the technical process of transforming inputs into outputs. If this producing part of the company operates ineffectively, it may offset economies in costs of inputs that have been achieved by effective procurement specialists, with the result that total costs per unit of output are inflated and thus influence prices that can be charged for outputs. It is therefore necessary that the type and structure of specialist areas in production departments are appropriate to the technical processes available. The aim must be to transform inputs into outputs in ways which, when all expenses have been met, will allow the creation of a surplus large enough to ensure the future purchase and renewal of the technologies required for production, such as machinery, buildings, systems, human skills and qualities, and material resources.

As we have seen from the work of Woodward and others, patterns of specialization appropriate for one technology could well be inappropriate to others. An organization structure for a capital-intensive chemical plant will not necessarily be appropriate for a vehicle assembly plant; logically, there must be an appropriate structure for each type of technology. Clearly, on the 'boundaries' of the transformation (production) function lie the output and input functions. The requirements of the client have to be conveyed to those who manage the production processes, and someone has to specialize in the translation of those requirements into raw materials and components, demands and specifications, and production schedules. The production schedules and the physical and human resources available are the parameters for the design of the work-flow from input to output, and the work flow requirements specify the job requirements which in their turn specify the labour-market requirement, which is signalled to those responsible for the recruitment of people from outside, and the deployment of people inside the organization.

Decisions as to the appropriate structure of specialist areas and departments to be directly or indirectly involved in the transformation process will depend on such factors as the geographic layout of the production processes, the design of the machinery and the work stations, and what is included in the operator's task. For example, it is possible to make operators responsible for the quality of what they produce, which means that operators become quality controllers; this reduces the need for a separate department of quality control specialists or at least changes the function of such a department. The same considerations apply when one considers methods, engineering, and work measurement. Again, the choice amongst alternative structural patterns will hinge on criteria of the effectiveness of the whole transformation process. Which pattern of specialization would be appropriate could be judged according to the effect of each on the unit cost of the output. The procedure for planning beneficial changes described on page 114 ff. would assist this judgement. The end result of this analysis would be to add to the list of appropriate specialist areas and departments for our company something like the following:

1. Several production departments at each stage of the work flow, or for each product, or both.
2. Several production support departments dealing with production scheduling and control, methods, quality control, etc.
3. Stores and materials handling.
4. Warehouse for finished product.

The procedure just described defines the required structure of specialization, and is the starting point of organization design. To the extent that each department refines and pursues exclusively its own special competence, more or less severe problems of overall organ-

izational effectiveness could arise. The well-being of the organization may demand a high degree of coordination between some
specialized departments. For instance, if a marketing department
has in mind only the satisfaction of the demands of particular customers it might demand from production departments a degree of
product variety which would push costs to a point which, when
reflected in price, would be more than customers are prepared to
pay. Between two departments such as this there is obviously a
high requirement of coordination. Similarly, it does not make
much sense to plan production in such a way as to put a premium
on certain skills which are not, in the short term, available in the
labour market, even if from a narrow production perspective it
might seem to be the best way. There might not, on the face of it,
be such a strong need for coordination between a department
specializing in political lobbying and one which licenses technical
processes, although it is quite possible to envisage circumstances in
which the need would be high. The protection of the best interests
of the organization from the consequences of departmental sub-
optimization calls for appropriate structures and processes of
coordination. The exact requirement for coordination arises from
the required structure of specialization.

However, the mere existence of a required structure of specialization is not the only reason for the search for appropriate means
of coordination. The state of affairs in the environment of each
specialized department will probably differ with respect to such
matters as rate of change, the amount and quality of information
available, and the time that elapses after action has been taken
before the consequences are known. Social science research has
discovered, as we know, that non-hierarchical, non-bureaucratic,
adaptable organic structures are more appropriate in coping with
high rates of change, low certainty of information and long time-
spans of feedback. Hierarchical bureaucratic structures are more
appropriate to certainty, stability and short time-spans. We would
also expect that the two types of structure would be associated with
different attitudes and styles. Differences in special skills and
professional mysteries in departments, added to different structures
and styles, can make coordination that much more difficult, and
hence call for special attention to the need for appropriate methods
of coordination.

We can adapt the ideas of Lawrence and Lorsch to arrive at an estimate of the strength of the requirement for coordination arising from required specialization.

In Table 4 below, some characteristics of environments are listed. Opposite each one is a scale with 9 points. Each specialist department can be given a score representing its position with respect to each environmental characteristic. To simplify, we have taken five specialist areas – marketing and sales (M.S.), production (Prod.), purchasing (Pur.), political relations (Pol.), and personnel (Per.). For illustrative purposes we have placed each specialist area

Characteristics of environment		1	2	3	4	5	6	7	8	9	
Rate of change	LOW		Prod	Pur		Per			M.S.	Pol	HIGH
Certainty of information	HIGH		Prod	Pur		Per		Pol	M.S.		LOW
Time-span of feedback	SHORT		Prod		Pol	Pur	Per	M.S.			LONG

			Max.
Production : Marketing and Sales	= 7 + 7 + 6 =	20^s	27
Production : Purchasing	= 2 + 2 + 4 =	8^s	,,
Production : Personnel	= 4 + 4 + 5 =	13^s	,,
Production : Political Relations	= 8 + 6 + 3 =	17^w	,,
Marketing : Political Relations	= 2 + 2 + 4 =	8^m	,,
Marketing : Purchasing	= 6 + 6 + 3 =	15^m	,,
Marketing : Personnel	= 4 + 4 + 2 =	10^m	,,
Purchasing : Personnel	= 3 + 3 + 2 =	8^w	,,
Purchasing : Political Relations	= 7 + 5 + 2 =	14^s	,,
Political Relations : Personnel	= 5 + 3 + 3 =	11^m	,,
		124	270

s = strong coordination requirement
w = weak coordination requirement
m = medium coordination requirement

Table 4 Calculating the requirement for coordination

at a point on the scale. The coordination requirement between departments can be judged by reference to the distance between the positions of each pair of departments on the scales. The requirement may, of course, be less than the scale scores indicate if it is judged that specialized departments have little effect on each other so that different structures and styles do not matter much.

Before we move on to consider how the coordination requirement identified by Table 4 can be met, it is necessary to stress the relationship of characteristics, structure and style on the one hand, and the characteristics of the environment on the other, which have already been briefly referred to. The efficient and effective mode of response to an environment with low rates of change, high certainty of information and short time-span of feedback is a bureaucratic mode where structures are rigid and hierarchical procedures are highly routine and roles and specialized functions are well defined. The styles of behaviour which fit the bureaucratic mode are a concern for the continuity of existing departments, high formality and defensiveness in personal relationships, deference to formal authority and a dislike of radical change. As rates of change increase, as information becomes less certain, and time-spans of feedback lengthen, continuing efficiency and effectiveness demand more flexible, adaptive structures and styles (for example, less concern with formal position and more concern with the immediate task, an acceptance of change as the normal state of affairs, the replacement of hierarchical structures and hermetically sealed specialist departments with flat networks of cooperating colleagues). We have described this set of characteristics as organic, following Burns. Of course, if the operational exigencies of a particular organization require little interaction between two specialist departments, it matters little whether their structures and styles are compatible. Where high interaction is required and structures and styles differ, then the incompatibilities become of practical concern as a factor inhibiting efficiency and effectiveness.

Having specified the need for coordination between specialist areas and departments, it is necessary to find structures and procedures for coordination to match that need. Generally speaking, a low need for coordination can be met by simple structures and procedures. A small company manufacturing a single, standard product for a small range of customers, which employs a simple production technology and procures a small range of easily accessible materials and components, probably needs only a shallow, formal chain of command through which the wishes of the chief executive can be conveyed, and some elementary control systems that will allow outcomes to be checked against intentions, and provide information to back decisions. To employ more elaborate structures and procedures would be a waste of effort, since the pattern of specialization is fairly primitive and there will be little difference in the structures and styles of rudimentary specialist departments. Of course, if the company grows, enters new and risky markets, adopts complex technology to produce new ranges of products which need different and more varied materials and components, then its coordinating 'mechanisms' will have to be supplemented. Usually in such cases committees are set up to bring together specialist managers, and managers from different organization levels, to address general problems of the organization rather than the particular problems of specialists, and to find ways of harnessing specialized knowledge and skill to these general problems and purposes. As the environment of an organization becomes differentiated with respect to rates of change, information certainty and time-span of feedback, and new specialist areas are created and special departments established, each adopting appropriate structures and styles, the need for coordination increases. To the extent that the need goes unrecognized, so the ability of the organization to cope effectively with the changes taking place in its environment will decrease. Enough is known of the ways in which organizations have responded to uncertain, more rapidly changing environments and increasingly complex technologies to make possible a hypothesis relating the need for coordination to the means that are available to meet that need. The list below shows, in descending order, the means frequently introduced in response to more complex and differentiated patterns of specialization. They are additive – committees do not replace formal organization and simple controls, but supplement them, and organizational development is introduced in addition to everything else. Obviously, however, the addition of new procedures affects the operation of those introduced earlier.

Some organizations 'rotate' younger managers through various specialist departments to make sure that they become 'generalists' with sufficient knowledge of the problems of specialized departments other than their own to enable them eventually to appreciate their point of view. The Lawrence and Lorsch studies suggest that this might serve to dilute the dedication of specialists to their

MEANS OF COORDINATION	DESCRIPTION
1 Personal influence	Proprietor/manager coordinates personally, relying on informal reporting from below and personal communication down.
1 + 2 Formal organization	Emerging specialist areas coordinated by formal reporting procedures; roles and responsibilities more formally defined.
1 + 2 + 3 Control procedures	Formal and impersonal procedures for control of production, control of costs, etc.
1 + 2 + 3 + 4 Committees	Influence of senior managers exercised through committees where specialists discuss organizational problems and the role of specialist departments in solving them.
1 + 2 + 3 + 4 + 5 Liaison persons/departments; task forces and project teams	Persons linking marketing and production, for example, to prevent damaging conflicts. Mobilization of different specialists to find solutions to cross-specialist problems, for example energy conservation, salary structures, new product development.
1 + 2 + 3 + 4 + 5 + 6 Matrix structures	Structures whose express aim is coordination. Matrices could include 'line' and 'functional' managers or product managers and specialist support departments.
1 + 2 + 3 + 4 + 5 + 6 + 7 Organization development	Procedures especially designed to cope with the need for changing attitudes, styles, to seek common ways of operating and to focus effort on the solution of tasks of high organizational priority.

Table 5 Means of coordination

specialist tasks. The lesson to be learned seems to be that it is better to have efficient specialists and good coordinating mechanisms than the worst of both worlds, although there may be some point in everyone having a good general appreciation of everyone else's specialist areas. Many management courses in companies and in business schools have that as their aim; it seems a sensible adjunct to specialized professional training, and a preparation for those senior management posts which demand some knowledge of all the specialist areas and are assigned some responsibility for coordinating them.

Referring back now to Table 4, we can propose that when the 'difference scores' are low between few specialist areas with a low coordination need, we will need only the coordination mechanisms at the top of our list. As the 'difference scores' increase between many specialist areas with high coordination need, we will need more and more of the mechanisms in order to respond with high performance to a complex environment.

Although we have illustrated the procedure derived from Lawrence and Lorsch by reference to new organization design, it can also be used without much amendment as a diagnostic check on an established organization to identify gaps in coordination and to close them, or to destructure specialist activities.

Dimensions of organization

The work of Pugh *et al.* (1963), we have already noted, is built on three distinguishable theoretical foundations. Firstly, the work of Lupton and his associates, which, from factual evidence about differences in worker behaviour in different industrial settings, speculated about the organizational and environmental factors apparently causing such differences. Secondly, Weber's procedure for distinguishing ideal types of organization. Thirdly, Pugh and his colleagues also drew on their knowledge of the procedures of definition and measurement used by psychologists to distinguish one complex individual person from another to help them in the task of constructing organizational profiles.

This group distinguished, quite early in their investigations, four distinct but interrelated levels of organization, namely:

1. The environment.
2. The formal structure of relationships of authority and control.
3. The groupings of persons in and around the formal structure by their common interest, background and shared beliefs.
4. The individual.

147

They assumed that the formal structure of authority and sub-ordination, and the administrative procedures for controlling the processes of production in any organization, would arise from that organization's efforts to adapt to its environment at some period of time. In turn, the structure and procedures would create the setting in which group affiliations would emerge. In turn, membership of groups would have a powerful effect on the behaviour of individuals. Two things follow:

1. That the chains of causation that result in individual behaviour run in from the environment via structure and group.
2. It ought to be possible in detail to classify environments, structures, groupings and individual behaviour, and then to suggest in the first place what structures and patterns of group behaviour are commonly found to be related to what environments, and second, what structure *ought* to go with what environments if a particular organization is to adapt effectively to its particular environment.

To date, the outstanding contribution of Pugh and his colleagues has been to define operationally a number of characteristics of organizational structure, e.g. centralization, decentralization, specialization and standardization, and to construct scales that can be used to score any organization on each dimension. This is a highly refined quantitative method for comparing the structure of organizations as diverse as hospitals, local-government departments, schools and engineering factories. Work is now going ahead to develop similar procedures to compare environments and behaviour in organizations. At the same time the search goes on for refined methods of measuring organizational performance. When all this is done it ought to be possible in a precise way to produce answers for managers who ask questions like:

How can we describe, and classify in quantitative terms, the kind of organization we have at present?
How can we do the same for the environment in which we operate?
How can we describe in detail the differences between the organizations we have and organization we *ought* to have, if we are to perform more effectively in the environment?
Along what dimensions is the environment likely to change?
What structural changes need to be made to adapt to environmental shifts?

How are these structural changes likely to affect behaviour, or rather what behavioural changes would make for the effective operation of a changed structure?

The Aston researchers have so far been more concerned to use the methods they have devised to refine theory and measurement and to do cross-national comparative work than to address practical questions, such as we have just listed. Nobody else, to my knowledge, has yet attempted to transform the Aston work into practical guidelines for organizational designers. Anyone who did so would see an immediate use of the measures of structure to draw 'profiles' of the structure of adjacent specialized units in the same organization to give some quantified impression of aspects of coordination requirement supplementing the procedure for organization design just outlined.

There is a possible criticism that both the work of Lawrence and Lorsch and of Pugh is too heavily weighted towards the structural determinist position in organization theory. From this standpoint, the behaviour of the individual in organizations is best explained by reference to the circumstances in which he finds himself, rather than by a reference to his personal characteristics, so that for example, the style of management or supervision that an organization might adopt – participation, authoritarian, etc. – would be more or less limited by circumstances.

Another plausible view, and one that we have dealt with in some detail already (page 95 ff.), would be that a particular style of management or supervision is best in all circumstances, in short, that the behaviour of individuals, which is susceptible to influence via education and training, and by systems of reward and sanction (although these are structural factors) is the dynamic factor in the structuring of organization relationships. This view is represented in the work of Blake and Likert and, to a lesser extent, McGregor. The difference between structural relativists like Lawrence and Lorsch and the psychological universalists in organization theory is not so much that one emphasizes the constraints upon the behaviour of the individual that arise from the organization circumstances he finds himself in, and the other the personal qualities of the individual. If this were all there were to it, I would not wish to bore the practical reader with what would be just another sterile academic controversy. The practical point of great significance is that if one accepts the standpoint of the structural relativist one will be mostly asking questions about 'best fit' because one will be seeking to influence behaviour in appropriate (i.e. adaptive) directions by defining a structure of authority and control that will best meet changing environmental demands, i.e. the structure would define the appropriate personal style. On this view there would be no warrant for asserting that there is a universally best style, say, of supervisory behaviour; one would say, rather, that out of all the possible styles that could be envisaged, this or that one is best for this particular situation out of all the possible situations that could be envisaged.

If, on the other hand, one accepts that personal style is the crucial factor, this must inevitably lead to the view that since organizations are made up of individuals, and relationships between them, then the way to influence the performance of the organization is to work on the individuals so that their personal style changes in ways that make for satisfactory and effective working organizational relationships. And one is also led to the view that *whatever the problems* an organization faces, and these *will* differ according to environment, technology, etc., they can be tackled in similar ways by changes in style of personal behaviour; so one is led in practice to prescribe generally – e.g. to advocate Theory Y, 9/9 management or management by objectives, System 4, job enlargement, job enrichment and so on.

It would be a foolish manager who accepted either view completely – and it is not too difficult, if one has not been conditioned too early and too effectively by the adherents of one school or the other, to make good practical use of both. One could, for example, ask questions about the *limits* that structural factors impose on choice of personal style. For example, it could be that there are certain very strict limits on the range of organizational alternatives open if one is to effectively run a small jobbing engineering shop in a highly competitive market when labour is scarce. If the choice of one rather than another makes possible a policy of participative supervision, job enlargement and enrichment, and one believes that people will derive more satisfaction and be more highly motivated, and will therefore contribute more willingly to the organization, then it is sensible to make that choice. In a large capital-intensive chemical plant, operating in monopolistic or oligopolistic competitive conditions, the range of organizational alternatives might well differ considerably, and equally so the limits on the choice of a structural alternative that will make possible the pursuit of high individual satisfaction as well as effective organizational adaptation and performance.

Both the structural and the psychological perspectives are useful as tools for organizational diagnosis. It is my own belief, however, that work such as that of Lawrence and Lorsch, and Pugh promises to restore the balance of emphasis when it has tipped so strongly towards the universal prescriptions of the psychological school. It is this belief that led me and my colleague Gowler to develop a practical procedure for selecting a payment system (1969). This procedure recognizes both the dynamic interplay of personal behaviour and the force of structural circumstances. The general procedure of finding a 'best fit' of payment system and circumstances has been taken further by Lupton and Bowey (1970), Lupton and Tanner (1980b) and Bowey (1982), and extended to cover salary structures and self-regulating pay structures, and to derive the slope of bonus curves.

Choosing a payment system

As we saw earlier (pp. 101–4) the debate about systems of payment for industrial work has almost always been conducted in terms of what one might call psychological universalism. That is to say, schools of thought may be distinguished, each holding to different theories about what it is that moves men to work hard and effectively. To simplify a complex matter we will say that there are two main schools. On the one hand there are those that have claimed that workers are wholly, or primarily, interested in cash, and on the other those who place the emphasis on the power of social obligation to motivate. Some admit that both motives are present, others might argue that the distinction is invalid or over simplified. But however elaborate the arguments and however heated the controversies, they have overwhelmingly been about what is the best system to suit all circumstances.

On the face of it, the proposition that all men everywhere, or at the very least men of western cultures, seek to satisfy the same general needs and predispositions, seems reasonable. The problem then becomes one of identifying the needs and predispositions (whether these be simple or complex) and using this knowledge as the basis for, *inter alia*, designing payment systems that will call forth hard and effective work. It is equally reasonable on the face of it to suppose that the design will not differ with the location of the individual in physical or social space, or with his relationship to technology as I have defined that term.

There have been some concessions to the view that circumstances might influence the way an individual regards the job he is doing, or the way the job affects his behaviour. For example, few people would push an argument for cash payment by results when the individual in question has no control over the results, so that his motives become largely irrelevant. The man on the assembly line has minimal control over the pace of work or even of the quality. He cannot determine the output of the finished component or car. So it makes little sense to offer payment by results, if the payment is intended to influence results *via* its effect on motives.

Once the search for circumstantial exceptions begins it must, in the nature of things, uncover more. Suppose one were to look at an engineering technology of a different kind to the example just referred to, e.g. small-batch production of products to customer's specification. The problems of administering such technologies are notoriously difficult, e.g. frequent stoppages of work for short periods due to faulty components, to set machines for a different run, or because all the parts are not at the right place at the right time, are examples of what often happens. Such stoppages might (usually will) give rise to claims to restore lost earnings when an individual is paid by the output of finished jobs or components. It's no fault of mine that the parts were not there on time, or the machines had to be reset, or that the assembly of a component was difficult, therefore I must not be expected to bear the risks – is a common argument of workers in such circumstances. Frequent changes of product can and will give rise to claims for a change in the price per piece or the performance standard.

Of course, such claims for adjustment of pay or performance to meet the circumstances are more likely to be met if the firm's market position is buoyant and labour is hard to come by or trades unions are strong, or both.* In short, the individual's behaviour, whatever we may suppose his motives to be, is the result of the interplay between his desires and predispositions on the one hand, and the constraints and opportunities in his immediate environment on the other. Managers are familiar with the phenomena of

---

* In short, the risks move, as it were, up and down the organization, as environmental changes shift the balance of power of the parties involved in adjusting pay or performance.

erosion or decay of incentive systems – and we have given examples of this process earlier – in which somehow the pulling power of the cash incentive has been reduced (or so it seems) by tight labour markets, strong unions engaged in leap frogging claims, and the high incidence of occasions for claims produced by the technology. For the engineering manager this will look like a familiar check-list of the common faults of payment-by-results systems.

But there are situations where PBR *succeeds* in motivating and when the circumstances do not erode it. There are also circumstances when the motive of social obligation present in some measured day-work systems (i.e. systems in which the pay is regular, but a certain measured performance is agreed as reasonable) is also eroded, and performance standards fall off while pay remains the same. There are also circumstances where measured day-work is reported as having been free from erosion of this kind for long periods in the history of a firm. Clearly, then, we do not have to be committed to a view that it is all psychological, nor do we have to believe the opposite, that motives have nothing to do with behaviour. We can equally say that, given clarity about objectives, it should be possible to choose from the payment systems available that which seems most likely, given the circumstances, to achieve those objectives.

So, instead of being committed to a belief about human motivation which only leads to conflict with those committed to other beliefs, we ought to ask: How can payment systems be classified in terms of the motivational principle which underlies them? Given that such a classification is possible, a method is needed for distinguishing one set of circumstances from another, and finally a procedure for finding the best fit possible between payment system and circumstance. Presently I shall outline how this may be systematically done. Before I do so I draw the reader's attention to the similarity between the reasoning behind this procedure, and that behind the work of Woodward, Burns, Lawrence and Lorsch, and Pugh. All these have implied that the performance of organizations is related to the match or fit of the way they structure the behaviour of their members, and the environment in which they operate. To identify the best fit is a complex procedure since environments are complex and differentiated, and subject to change. The method for selecting a payment system is a partial attempt to solve the best-fit puzzle. It shows how one adaptive procedure, i.e. the procedure for relating the effort and reward of

shop-floor operators, may be identified. My purpose is to emphasize the process of matching environment and procedure, and not
simply the choice of payment system. I am certain that similar procedures derived from a systems view of organization will soon follow. Why, for example, can we not choose a system of financial
control that is a best fit, or a pattern of distributing authority, or
a system of job grading and pay differentials?

Since this was first written, a contingent view of financial control
systems *is* now at last beginning to emerge (McCosh *et al.*, 1982)
and, as already mentioned, a contingent procedure for designing
salary structures now exists. The procedure for choosing a payment
system comprises a method of drawing a situation profile along
twenty-three dimensions, some technological, some relating to
labour markets, some about occupational structure and power, and
some about the age and sex characteristics of the labour force. The
profiling procedure seems capable of finely distinguishing one
situation from another on these particular dimensions. The profile
dimensions represent a system; if the product market changes,
technology might also alter in response, and these might create new
skills for which there is no supply in the labour market. Thus the
profile of any one plant or workshop may change from time to
time.

The classification of payment systems is based upon a definition
which describes them as sets of rules and procedures relating some
kind of effort to some kind of reward. The procedure for choosing
from the payment systems represented in the classification the one
which best matches the situation profile is somewhat lengthy and
complex, and the reader is referred to Lupton and Gowler (1969)
if he wishes to master it in detail. The principle is simplicity itself
and is easily exemplified.

One of the technological dimensions is length of job cycle, that
is, the time it takes for someone to take up a job, complete it, and
lay it down finished. Short-job cycle work is usually unskilled
repetitive work. Long-job cycle work is usually skilled, responsible
work. Other things being equal, cash PBR systems are best suited
to repetitive work; so if the score on a particular firm's profile for
length of job cycle were low our procedure would choose for *that
firm on that dimension* a PBR scheme. The scores might indicate
that on other dimensions (say operator discretion or labour stability) a time-rate system or a group-bonus system might be a good
fit. From the whole analysis it is possible to deduce what particular

combinations of motivational principles would best suit the circumstances as described by the profile. These principles can then be used to design a system of payment.

This procedure takes account of motives other than cash which influence behaviour, by showing how the shape of a situation profile may be altered to take account of them; and it can also be used to show that elements in a situation may have to be changed and by how much, if an *existing* payment system is to be less liable to erosion and decay.

The technology of reconciliation

In Chapter 4 we referred to the ideas of Herzberg and raised some doubts about how widely his generalizations about the causes and consequences of job satisfaction applied in practice. We also remarked that the movement to improve the quality of life at work, although still very much alive in the realm of ideas, has been slowed down in its application by depressed economic conditions. There is little doubt that there will be a resurgence and that some managers will be persuaded by market pressure, public clamour, trade-union pressure, or availability of investment funds, to design, install and manage flexible manufacturing systems as humanely as possible, without sacrificing technical and economic efficiency. Indeed, the practical question for the manager who wishes for one reason or another to provide enriched tasks for workers is: How far can I go with it and still remain efficient and competitive?

What kind of job offers a rich quality of life at work? A detached middle-class observer might well define such a job as an interesting, challenging, responsible and secure one, full of variety and choice, located in a clean, bright and safe workplace, and offering opportunities to the occupant of it to be involved in decisions affecting his well-being. An impoverished job, our observer might say, would show the opposite set of characteristics. Would that it were as simple as that, and that the motivation of workers always varied directly with the quality of the job as defined here. All that would be required then would be to design manufacturing systems full of enriched jobs, and high production efficiency would follow by way of the heightened motivation of satisfied workers.

However, there is no necessary connection between enriched jobs *à la* Herzberg on the one hand and production efficiency on the other, because the costs of designing, installing and running a manufacturing system full of enriched jobs could, in certain circumstances (the nature of which will presently be specified), be prohibitively costly, and also because the worker's own definition of a satisfying job might be very different from that of our middle-class observer and equally might differ from worker to worker. If one is designing a manufacturing system with worker satisfaction in mind, it makes sense to make sure firstly that it is capable of making a good quality product at a cost that makes it competitive in the market place, and secondly that the jobs created by the system are going to be satisfying to the actual workers involved and not necessarily designed to the specification of our middle-class observer. The problem of design is to match the real preferences of those who will operate the technical system with the technical system itself, and so effect a reconciliation in practice between the economic, technical, sociological and psychological, and embody it fully into the design.

The following is a brief description of an actual design exercise carried out in an engineering assembly plant by a team comprising engineers and social scientists, during which a procedure for reconciliation was evolved using open socio-technical system approaches and also some methods drawn from social-science research (Lupton, 1975).

Visualize a complex product involving the assembly of hundreds of parts, some large enough to require mechanical handling, others as small as minute screws. The product is sold on a mass world market, and the daily output on two shifts is about 1,000. The product is manufactured on a traditional assembly line employing 160 workers. Parts are moved from work station to work station by overhead conveyor belts and chains. Each operator has to remain at his work station, to which bins of small parts are attached, until the job is conveyed to him. He then has to complete the assembly operation within a specified, short-cycle time, after which the job moves on to the next work station in the sequence. Various versions of the same basic product are manufactured on the line, which necessitates some variations in components and operations and hence in job requirements. This means that from time to time some workers have to be moved around on the line.

The management is contemplating the construction of a completely new line with much the same capacity. The design considerations are:

1. Machinery now exists that would perform some operations mechanically that are currently performed manually.
2. Trade-union power has increased. The unions are pressing for cleaner, lighter, and safer working conditions.
3. Management wishes to go along with the current trend toward job enrichment and job enlargement, not only because of public and union pressure, but also because of a sincere desire to be progressive and do the right thing by their workers.
4. The rate of growth of the world market for the product has declined, and competition will become fiercer within the next few years, not only in design and quality but also in price.
5. It will become increasingly difficult to recruit workers to work on the existing line.

Specifications for the new line are given to a project team requiring them to create a design which will produce a high volume of quality products of good design at low cost; provide working conditions that are quiet, safe, light and airy; provide enriched/enlarged jobs for workers; and use machinery to replace labour whenever possible on the production operations. The specifications themselves immediately raised the question whether, or to what extent, all the objectives could be achieved simultaneously.

The project team followed a systematic procedure which began by examining all the alternative ways that could be thought of to assemble the product, and they turned out to be:

1. A single operator would assemble the whole product from its component parts – that is, there would be a number of individual work stations to which the components would be delivered and from which finished products would be collected.
2. A single operator would assemble a significant part of the product – that is, there would be a large group of operations and components providing long-cycle, varied work. Components would be delivered to the work stations and the sub-assemblies conveyed from station to station.
3. Small groups of workers would assemble the whole product. The arrangements for delivery of parts to and collection of products from work stations would be similar to the first alternative. The detailed arrangements for the organization of work would be left to the workers themselves.
4. Small groups of workers would assemble a significant part of the product, enough to make a long, interesting cycle of operations

and product opportunities for job rotation within the group. The arrangements for delivery and sequencing would be the same as in the second alternative.

5. Work stations, as in the existing system, would be placed in line, and parts would be delivered continuously by conveyors to the work stations. Some manual pacing of work would be possible.
6. A completely planned assembly line would be created; speed and manning would be determined by the speed of machines and conveyors, i.e. an updated mechanized version of the existing line.

If the quality of work had not been a factor, the team would probably have opted early on, for reasons of cost and management control, for a combination of the fifth and sixth alternatives, that is, it would have introduced completely mechanized sections of the line using recently developed machines that would set the operator's pace, and then design the other sections according to the pattern of the existing line. The instructions, however, specified quiet, safe, light and airy working conditions along with enriched and enlarged jobs. On first inspection it looked as if the alternatives scoring high on business efficiency (the fifth and sixth alternatives) would score lowest on the quality of work. The implications of some of the other alternatives were not clear-cut and had to be examined more carefully. To make this possible, it is necessary to have a procedure that discriminates according to quality of work dimensions as accurately as the procedures that were used to discriminate according to cost and control. The procedure measured and compared the kinds of jobs required by each of the six work systems. The categories used to measure the job requirements were also used to measure the job preferences of the workers. The best 'match' of 'job profile' and 'preference profile' indicated which of the six work systems was closest to the workers' own preferences. This was then evaluated according to technical and economic criteria to see whether and by how much it fell short of the specification. Then the search was on amongst the six work systems for the one which gave the best balance of economic, social, technical and psychological aims, consistent with the survival and development of the organization.

The five categories for measuring job requirements and job preferences were derived from Turner and Lawrence (1965). They are:

1. *Variety* of tools used and parts assembled.

2. *Autonomy* – the degree of freedom available to workers to organize their own tasks, vary their workplace, change duties with others, correct errors without supervision and preassemble job components.
3. *Responsibility* for reaching production targets without mechanical pacing or close supervision, for high-quality work, and towards others within a work group.
4. *Interaction* – the degree of opportunity for social contact within work groups (a function of the size of the group, the location of people in it, and the layout of the workplace), and freedom to arrange work schedules by group decision.
5. *Completeness of task* – the degree to which the finished job is a recognizable entity to which workers can attach some significance and take some pride in.

A nine-point scale was developed for each factor and rules were established for allocating a score on each for the jobs associated with the alternative manufacturing systems. The engineers' knowledge of the way the total assembly operation was divided on the existing line – the tools used, the parts required, the location of work stations, and so on – was invaluable as a basis for indicating how scores on the scales might be allocated when these elements were put together differently. Both the engineers and the social scientists also had seen or were familiar with examples of manufacturing systems for similar products that resembled some of the various alternatives. All in all, it was not too difficult to secure agreement among the investigators and the managers of the plant themselves on the job profiles.

After examining these profiles it would have been easy to rule some of them out immediately, using quality of work criteria. However, the purpose of the project was to satisfy not only quality of work criteria but also technical efficiency and commercial criteria. There was also a requirement to look for opportunities to employ machines instead of people. Neither was it appropriate to ignore the values, expectations, concerns – in short, the job preferences – of those who would have to make the new manufacturing system work.

Once job-requirement profiles had been completed, the social scientists suggested several ways that could be used to help profile job expectations using the very same five factors. First, workers on the existing assembly line, or a sample of them, would be interviewed. The questions would be carefully designed to encourage people to evaluate their present jobs against jobs they had previously done themselves and had seen others doing. Second, they recommended making detailed observations of behaviour on the existing line in order to discover to what extent the designed tasks, sequences, and work-station locations were being altered or ignored by the operators. On the assumption that individuals will alter their environment as far as possible to reflect their preferences, the alterations would indicate the nature of these preferences. For example, unplanned job-swapping might be interpreted as an indication of a desire for more variety, more control and more frequent personal interaction. The foremen, all of whom were ex-workers, were to be asked to indicate their opinion of worker preferences, and so were a number of managers and engineers. It was not possible in this case to interview workers, and their profiles were constructed from the social scientists' observations.* The three sets of profiles were somewhat different, but not wildly so, the workers' preferences for job enrichment as conventionally defined being weaker than the others thought they would be. The process of profile-matching revealed that alternative 4 was nearest to the preferences of the work force and would also satisfy the technical and economic performance criteria. The chosen alternative posed some technical problems when detailed layouts came to be drawn, and a compromise was agreed which would create a larger number of impoverished jobs than was originally envisaged.

The engineers on this project found that their engineering skills and ingenuity were severely tested by the necessity of finding technical solutions within constraints imposed by quality-of-work considerations. The social scientists found it equally testing to be confronted with physical and cost limitations on social and psychological approaches to job design. However, if the open socio-technical system idea is to be given practical expression, the design teams, whether they are designing payment systems, organization structures, factory layouts, or human satisfaction, must include members whose specialist areas correspond to the various elements of an open socio-technical system, and all must be familiar with the idea and confident enough to turn it to practical use.

---

* Interviews are in general recommended not least because they give workers a feeling that they are in some way involved in the process of design.

There are other published examples of reconciliation technologies, and I refer to three of these. The first two are concerned with manufacturing systems, and the third with information technology.

Engineers and personnel specialists in a French manufacturing company evolved a complex system for designing work stations which became standard practice for engineers in the company and was embodied in a manual which was later published for a wider audience (Lucas, 1976). The method includes a profile-matching procedure. Almost simultaneously, a similar procedure was being evolved in a large German company which featured employee involvement in articulating preferences to be incorporated into a complex matching technique (Metzger, Schafer and Zippe, 1975).

A similar method of designing workplaces, developed to be used especially when new information technology is being introduced into offices, obtains information from employees about their needs and preferences by means of questionnaires. This information is then examined and analysed by groups which include the workers themselves. From this analysis are derived some 'social objectives' for the new work system. There will already be some technical objectives for the proposed new systems and the method involves a joint effort by workers, managers and technical specialists to find, within cost and resource constraints, a work system which will give the best 'match' of social and technical objectives. This ETHICS method (Effective Technical and Human Implementation of Computer Systems) has been used quite widely and some examples of its practical application, together with a description of the method and a procedure for monitoring results, are reported in Mumford and Weir (1979).

These few examples of the practical implications of organization theory for management take us forward a great deal from the position of being in a general way attracted by open-system views of organization, to the point when practical procedures based on them are now possible or actually in existence. I predict that when we learn better how to derive these procedures, and when managers accustom themselves to the ideas that lie behind them, much that now remains in the sphere of ideology and guesswork will be raised to the level of scientific discourse and technological know-how, and human relationships in industry will be the better for it, not to speak of economic efficiency.

My only regret is that progress is so slow, and that it will continue to be so until more social scientists turn more of their attention to practical matters, and more managers take an interest in potentially useful theories and try to give them practical form, working towards a meeting of minds on matters of mutual concern. The lead will, I suspect, have to continue to come from social scientists and I hope that this book and its point of view will be seen as a modest step in that direction.

References

AGUREN, S., and EDGREN, J. (1980), *New Factories*, Swedish Employers Federation, Stockholm.

ARGYRIS, C. (1957), *Personality and Organization*, Harper & Row.

BARNARD, C. (1948), *The Functions of the Executive*, Harvard University Press.

BLAKE, R. R., and MOUTON, J. S. (1961), *The Managerial Grid*, Gulf Publishers.

BOWEY, A. (ed.) (1982), *Handbook of Wage and Salary Systems*, Gower Press.

BOYATZIS, R. E. (1982), *The Competent Manager*, Wiley.

BROWN, W. (1960), *Explorations in Management*, Heinemann.

BURNS, T., and STALKER, G. M. (1961), *The Management of Innovation*, Tavistock.

CARLSON, S. (1951), *Executive Behaviour: A Study of the Work Load and Working Methods of Managing Directors*, Strombergs, Stockholm.

CUNNISON, S. (1965), *Wages and Work Allocation*, Tavistock.

CYERT, R. M., and MARCH, J. G. (1963), *A Behavioral Theory of the Firm*, Prentice-Hall.

DUBIN, R. (1962), *Human Relations in Administration*, Prentice-Hall. (This is a collection of many of the best readings in the social sciences of management. The linking commentary by Dubin is of great value.)

FAYOL, H. (1949), *General and Industrial Administration*, Pitman.

FLANDERS, A. (1964), *The Fawley Productivity Agreements*, Faber.

FRIEDMANN, G. (1955), *Industrial Society*, Free Press.

GLUCKMAN, M. (ed.) (1964), *Closed Systems and Open Minds*, Oliver & Boyd.

GOLDTHORPE, J. H., LOCKWOOD, D., BECHHOFER, F., and PLATT, J. (1968), *The Affluent Worker: Industrial Attitudes and Behaviour*, Cambridge University Press.

GOULDNER, A. W. (1955a), *Patterns of Industrial Bureaucracy*, Routledge & Kegan Paul.

GOULDNER, A. W. (1955b), *Wildcat Strike*, Routledge & Kegan Paul.

GRAY, A. P., and ABRAMS, M. (1954), *Construction of Esso Refinery, Fawley: A Study in Organization*, British Institute of Management.

HERZBERG, F., MAUSNER, B., and SNYDERMAN, B. B. (1959), *The Motivation to Work*, Wiley.

HOMANS, G. C. (1951), *The Human Group*, Routledge & Kegan Paul.

HORNE, J. H., and LUPTON, T. (1965), 'The Work Activities of Middle Managers – an exploratory study', *J. Manag. Stud.*, vol. 2, pages 14–33.

HUMBLE, J. (1969), *Management by Objectives*, Industrial Educational Research Foundation.

ISHIKAWA, K. (ed.) (1958), *QC Circle Activities*, Union of Japanese Scientists and Engineers, Tokyo.

JAQUES, E. (1951), *The Changing Culture of a Factory*, Tavistock.

JAQUES, E. (1956), *The Measurement of Responsibility*, Tavistock.

KEPNER, C. H. and TREGOE, B. B. (1973), *The Rational Manager: A Systematic Approach to Problem Solving and Decision Making.* McGraw-Hill, London.

KOONTZ, H. (1966), 'Making theory operational: the span of management', *J. Manag. Stud.*, vol. 3, no. 3, pages 229–43.

LAWRENCE, P. R., and LORSCH, J. W. (1967), *Organization and Environment*, Harvard Graduate School of Business Administration.

LEWIN, K. (1951), *Field Theory in Social Science*, Tavistock.

LIKERT, R. (1967), *The Human Organization*, McGraw-Hill.

LUCAS, A. (1976), *Les Profils de Postes*, Sirtes and Masson, Paris.

LUPTON, T. (1963), *On the Shop Floor*, Pergamon.

LUPTON, T. (1966), *Industrial Behaviour and Personnel Management*, Institute of Personnel Management.

LUPTON, T. (1975), 'Efficiency and the Quality of Worklife – the Technology of Reconciliation', *Organisation Dynamics*, Autumn 1975, pages 68–79.

LUPTON, T., BERRY, A. J., and WARMINGTON, A. (1977), 'The Contribution of a Business School to a Joint Development Activity', *Management Education and Development*, vol. 7, pages 2–12.

LUPTON, T., and BOWEY, A. (1970), 'Productivity Drift and the Structure of the Pay Packet', *J. Manag. Stud.*, vol. 7, pages 151–71, 310–34.

LUPTON, T., and GOWLER, D. (1969), *Selecting a Wage Payment System*, Engineering Employers Federation Research Paper no. 3.

LUPTON, T., and TANNER, I. (1980a), 'Work Design in Europe', in Duncan K. D. *et al.* (eds.) *Changes in Working Life*, Wiley.

LUPTON, T., and TANNER, I. (1980b), 'A Self-regulating Pay Structure at Plant Level, *Personnel Review*, vol. 9, pages 21–6.

LUPTON, T., and TANNER, I. (1981), 'Organisational Change for Productivity Improvement', *Proc. International Conference European Federation of Productivity Services, Zurich.*

LUPTON, T., WARMINGTON, A., and CLAYTON, T. (1974), 'Organisational Development at Pilkingtons', *Personnel Review*, vol. 3, pages 4–7.

MARCH, J. G. and SIMON, H. A. (1958), *Organizations*, Wiley.

MARPLES, D. L. (1967), 'Studies of Managers – A fresh start?', *J. Manag. Stud.*, vol. 4, pages 282–99.

MCCOSH, A., WHITING, E. A., and HOWELLS, S. (1982), Research and Planning Control under Inflation, Unpublished research report – Manchester Business School.

MCGREGOR, D. (1960), *The Human Side of Enterprise*, McGraw-Hill.

MERTON, R. K. (1957), *Social Theory and Social Structure*, Free Press.

METZGER, H., SCHAFER, A., and ZIPPE, H. (1975), 'Methode zur Bewertung von Arbeitsystemen', in *Arbeitsstrukturiering in der Deutschen Metallindustrie*, pages 22–31, Institut für Angewandte Arbeitswissenschaft, Cologne.

MILLWARD, N. (1968), 'Family status and behaviour at work', *Sociol. Rev.*, vol. 16, no. 2, pages 149–64.

MINTZBERG, H. (1973), *The Nature of Managerial Work*, Harper & Row.

MUMFORD, E., and WEIR, M. (1979), *Computer Systems in Work Design – the ETHICS method*, Associated Business Press.

MYERS, C. S. (1933), *Industrial Psychology in Great Britain*, Cape.

PUGH, D. S., HICKSON, D. J., HININGS, C. R., McDONALD, K. M., TURNER, C., and LUPTON, T. (1963), 'A conceptual scheme for organizational analysis', *Admin. Sci. Q.*, vol. 8, no. 3, pages 288–315.

REVANS, R. W. (1980), *Action Learning: New Techniques for Management*, Blond and Briggs.

RICE, A. K. (1958), *Productivity and Social Organisation*, Tavistock.

RICE, A. K. (1963), *The Enterprise and its Environment*, Tavistock.

ROETHLISBERGER, F. J., and DICKSON, W. J. (1939), *Management and the Worker*, Harvard University Press.

ROY, D. (1954), 'Efficiency and the fix', *Amer. J. Sociol.*, vol. 60, no. 3, pages 255–66.

SAYLES, L. (1958), *Behaviour in Industrial Work Groups*, Wiley.

SCOTT, W. H., BANKS, J., HALSEY, A. H., and LUPTON, T., (1956), *Technical Change and Industrial Relations*, Liverpool University Press.

SELZNICK, P. (1948), 'Foundations of the theory of Organisations', *Amer. Soc. Rev.*, vol. 13, pages 25–35.

SMITH, P., and HONOUR, T. F. (1969), 'The impact of phase one managerial grid training', *J. Manag. Stud.*, vol. 6, no. 3, pages 318–30.

STEWART, R. (1967), *Managers and their Jobs*, Macmillan.

TAYLOR, F. W. (1947), *Scientific Management*, Harper & Row.

TRIST, E. L., HIGGIN, G. W., MURRAY, H., and POLLOCK, A. B. (1963), *Organizational Choice*, Tavistock.

TURNER, A., and LAWRENCE, P. (1965), *Industrial Jobs and the Worker*, Harvard Division of Research.

URWICK, L. (1943), *The Elements of Administration*, Harper & Row.

VROOM, V. H., and YETTON, P. W. (1971), *Leadership and Decision-making*, Pittsburgh University Press.

WALKER, C. R., and GUEST, R. H. (1952), *The Man on the Assembly Line*, Harvard University Press.

WARMINGTON, A., GRIBBIN, C., and LUPTON, T. (1977), *Industrial Behaviour and Performance*, Macmillan.

WEBER, M. (1946), *From Max Weber: Essays in Sociology*, H. H. Gerth and C. W. Miles (eds.), Oxford University Press.

WICKENS, J. D. (1968), 'Management by objectives: an appraisal', *J. Manag. Stud.*, vol. 5, no. 3, pages 365–79.

WILSON, C. S. (1962), 'Production norms in factories', Unpublished Ph.D. thesis, Manchester University.

WINN, A. (1969), 'The laboratory approach to organization development: a tentative model of planned change', *J. Manag. Stud.*, vol. 6, no. 2, pages 155–66.

WOODWARD, J. (1959), *Management and Technology*, HMSO.

WOODWARD, J. (1965), *Industrial Organization*, Oxford University Press.

ZALEZNIK, A., CHRISTENSEN, C. R., and ROETHLISBERGER, F. J. (1958), *The Motivation, Productivity and Satisfaction of Workers: A Predictive Study*, Harvard Graduate School of Business Administration.

Further Reading

FOGARTY, M. P. (1963), *The Rules of Work*, Chapman.

GLUCKMAN, M. (1956), *Custom and Conflict in Africa*, Blackwell.

KATZ, D., and KAHN, R. L. (1966), *The Social Psychology of Organizations,* Wiley.

LEAVITT, H. J. (1956), *Managerial Psychology*, University of Chicago Press. (An elementary introduction to some findings of social science which are relevant to management. It is clearly and wittily written.)

LITTERER, J. A. (1963), *Organizations: Structure and Behavior*, Wiley. (Another collection of articles and selections from books, with a linking commentary.)

LUPTON, T. (1960), *Money for Effort*, HMSO.

MASSIE, J. L. (1964), *Essentials of Management*, Prentice-Hall. (This book describes mathematical techniques in a treatment suitable for the lay manager, and gives reference to more specialized books in the same field.)

The manager who wishes to follow the discussion on the issues raised in this book would be advised to start with this general list of books together with Brown (1960) and Dubin (1962), and then to move from them to more detailed field researches.

Index

FIND OUT MORE ABOUT
PENGUIN BOOKS

We publish the largest range of titles of any English language paperback publisher. As well as novels, crime and science fiction, humour, biography and large-format illustrated books, Penguin series include *Pelican Books* (on the arts, sciences and current affairs), *Penguin Reference Books, Penguin Classics, Penguin Modern Classics, Penguin English Library, Penguin Handbooks* (on subjects from cookery and gardening to sport), and *Puffin Books* for children. Other series cover a wide variety of interests from poetry to crosswords, and there are also several newly formed series – *Lives and Letters, King Penguin, Penguin American Library* and *Penguin Travel Library*.

We are an international publishing house, but for copyright reasons not every Penguin title is available in every country. To find out more about the Penguins available in your country please write to our U.K. office – Dept EP, Penguin Books Ltd, Harmondsworth, Middlesex UB7 0DA – unless you live in one of the following areas:

In the U.S.A.: Dept DG, Penguin Books, 299 Murray Hill Parkway, East Rutherford, New Jersey 07073.

In Canada: Penguin Books Canada Ltd, 2801 John Street, Markham, Ontario L3R 1B4.

In Australia: Marketing Department, Penguin Books Australia Ltd, P.O. Box 257, Ringwood, Victoria 3134.

In New Zealand: Marketing Department, Penguin Books (N.Z.) Ltd, P.O. Box 4019, Auckland 10.

In India: Penguin Overseas Ltd, 706 Eros Apartments, 56 Nehru Place, New Delhi 110019.